Lost Railroads of
New England

Lost Railroads

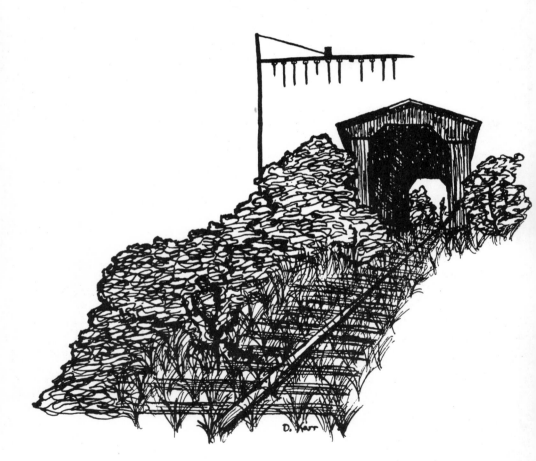

NEW ENGLAND RAIL HERITAGE SERIES

of

New England

Second Edition

RONALD DALE KARR

Branch Line Press

Pepperell, Massachusetts

Printed by Braum-Brumfield, Inc., Ann Arbor, MI, on recycled acid-free paper

Cover design and frontispiece by Diane B. Karr; cover art by Brian Beaudoin

Rear cover photo: *Abutments that once carried the B&M's Milford branch over a road in West Groton, Mass. The line was abandoned in 1941 (see line 166).*

All photos by the author except where noted

Library of Congress Card Number 95-76497
ISBN: 0-942147-04-9

Branch Line Press
13 Cross Street
Pepperell, Massachusetts 01463

10 9 8 7 6 5 4 3 2 1

To my Mother
and
in memory of my Father

Contents

Preface to the First Edition   9

Preface to the Second Edition   12

Maps   15

1   The Rise and Fall of New England's Railroads   33

2   The Saga of Lost Railroads   41

3   Finding Lost Railroads   65

4   Rail Abandonments in New England, 1848-1994   69

Bibliography   157

General Index   163

About the Author   167

The Nashua, Acton & Boston Railroad built this beautiful stone arch bridge in Westford, Mass., in 1872. More than seventy years have passed since its abandonment (see line 42).

Preface to the First Edition

ON MY WAY to work each morning I cross the rights of way of four railroads. Only one of these retains steel rails and wooden ties. The other three are ghost roads; with tracks removed, they are pathways of memories of cinders and steam. I reach the first forgotten rail line a block from my home. The path the railroad took is only faintly visible through the weeds and brush. The Boston and Maine abandoned these tracks on the eve of the Second World War. The wooden bridge that once carried the road over the tracks has long been removed and the cut filled in. Perhaps one person in a hundred notices the old right of way.

On the other side of town I come to a broad path of cinders cutting through the woods, unmistakably a railroad bed. The rails were pulled up by the B&M four years ago, but they might just as well have been lifted last week; the right of way seems to be awaiting their return. I sometimes see hikers, motorcyclists or bicyclists as my car drives over what was until recently a grade crossing.

Another five miles down the state highway I pass still a third lost railroad. On one side of the road the right of way has become a private jeep trail through the pines. On the other side the old rail bed is almost completely disguised by vegetation. Sixty years have passed since the last B&M locomotive plied this line.

A few ties and spikes are all that remain of this section of the former Milford branch of the B&M in Pepperell, Mass., in February 1996 (see line 146).

I live in Massachusetts, but my commute could be nearly anywhere in New England. The ruins of our region's railroading past are all around us: embankments in the woods, choked with weeds; foundations of forgotten bridges; ancient railroad depots miles from any extant tracks; street signs that proclaim "Railroad Avenue" and "Depot Street," where a locomotive's horn hasn't been heard in a generation.

Information on New England's lost railroads can be hard to come by. The only previous account of abandonments in the region was my *Rail Abandonments in New England, 1845-1981*, a list which I published in 1983. The list was assembled from a variety of sources, including the *Decisions of the Interstate Commerce Commission*, the listings of rail abandonments that have appeared in *Railway Age* and *Traffic World*, and various histories, maps, and articles. Readers of my first work will notice that many abandonments have been redated in light of better information.

It is often said that writing history is a collective endeavor, even if only a single author's name appears on the title page. This is certainly true of this work. A number of readers of my earlier work were kind enough to share their knowledge with me and point out where I had gone astray. I want to thank the following individuals for their comments, corrections, additions, and encouragement:

Stan DeOrsey, Poughkeepsie, N.Y.; Francis D. Donovan, Medway, Mass.; Charles H. Dunbar, Alexandria, Va.; Ron Fahnestock, Springfield, Pa.; John Gardner, South Burlington, Vt. Howard D. Goodwin, Wareham, Mass.; Edmund Hession, Boston, Mass.; David W. Jacobs, New York, N.Y.; Heiko Koester, Lexington, Mass.; Ray McCurdo, Waltham, Mass.; Dr. John P. Roberts, Transport Museum Association, St. Louis, Mo.; Dwight A. Smith, President, Conway Scenic Railroad, North Conway, N.H.; Richard W. Symmes, Curator, Walker Transportation Collection, Beverly (MA) Historical Society & Museum; H. Arnold Wilder, Boston & Maine Historical Society, Westford, Mass.; Roger Yepsen, Barto, Pa..

My former colleague, Mary Fortney, Map Librarian at the Northwestern University Library patiently endured my demands on her superb map collection and her geographical knowledge. Equally supportive were my fellow librarians at Northwestern University's Transportation Library, Dorothy Ramm and Mary MacCredie. Above all, my wife Diane has contributed to this project as editor and illustrator and in ways too numerous to recount.

Finally, any errors remain my responsibility. Despite my best efforts, a few have undoubtably crept in. I would greatly appreciate these being brought to my attention.

R.D.K.
Pepperell, Massachusetts
May 1987

Preface to the Second Edition

IN THIS NEW edition I have redrawn all of the maps and have expanded the abandonment list into a directory of rail abandonments. I retained the line numbers from the first edition, both to make it easier for readers of that book to follow and for me to keep track of them as well. A number of errors have been corrected and many lines omitted from the first edition have been added. Happily, most of my errors proved to be minor, the most common being the misdating of abandonments that occurred late in one year or early in the next.

As before, readers have contributed significantly to this effort. For correcting my mistakes and providing both information and encouragement I want to thank:

Mary Anthony, Pomfret Center, Conn.; Alfred S. Arnold, Holden, Mass.,; Edgar G. Bell, Littleton, Mass.; Dr. Edmund A. Bowles, Falls Church, Va.; Donald H. Brayden, Jr., Fitchburg, Mass.; R. C. Carpenter, East Norwalk, Conn.; R. Richard Conard, Wayland, Mass.; George Cook, Valatie, N.Y.; David S. Decker, Dayton, Ohio; Professor William L. Dills, University of Massachusetts Dartmouth; Seth Fisher, Tyngsboro, Mass.; John J. Gardner, Burlington, Vt.; Andrew H. Gaudet, Dallas, Tex.; Jack R. Gosselin, Putnam, Conn.; Richard N. Haywood, West Lafayette, Ind.; Andrew Held, Cambridge, Mass.; Paul Hotchkiss, Bethlehem, Conn.; John Kyper, Roxbury, Mass.; Frank J. Labuz, Palmer, Mass.; Nelson H. Lawry, Rollinsford, N.H.; Ray McMurdo, Waltham, Mass.; Robert E. Moran, Glastonbury, Conn.; Donald F. Morrison, Wallingford, Pa.; Professor

William E. O'Connell, Jr., College of William and Mary; Mathew D. Rines, Gorham, Me.; Donald S. Robinson, North Billerica, Mass.; Alan B. Rohwer, Boxborough, Mass.; William W. Schweikert, Mt.Hermon, Mass.; Henry E. Shea, Commack, N.Y.; David J. Texter, Manchester, N.H.; Rev. Carroll D. Tripp, Burlington, Vt.; Donald B. Valentine; Ellis E. Walker, Concord, Mass.; H. Arnold Wilder, Westford, Mass.

Special thanks are due to J. Leonard Bachelder of Merrimac, Mass., and Thomas J. Humphrey, of Waban, Mass., who provided extensive critiques and corrections. Marie Anne Drouin and Mary Beth McNeil, Interlibrary Loans, O'Leary Library, University of Massachusetts Lowell, kept me well supplied with source material. Martha Mayo, Special Collections Librarian, Center for Lowell History, University of Massachusetts Lowell provided access to the collections of the Boston & Maine Railroad Historical Society. Richard W. Symmes, Curator of the Walker Transportation Collection, Beverly Historical Society and Museum, helped provide a photograph.

As always, suggestions and comments are appreciated.

R.D.K.

December 1995

Maps

Built in 1911, the bridge that now carries U.S. Route 4 across the Quechee Gorge in Hartford, Vt., once bore the tracks of the Woodstock Railroad. After the short line closed down operations in 1933, this impressive steel arch was converted to highway use (see line 76).

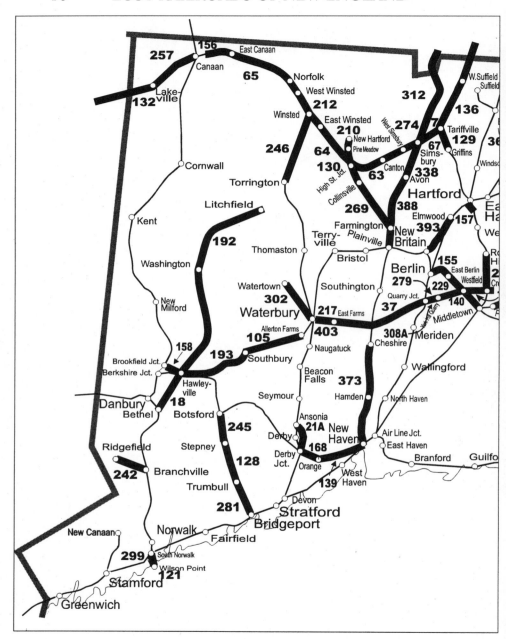

Connecticut

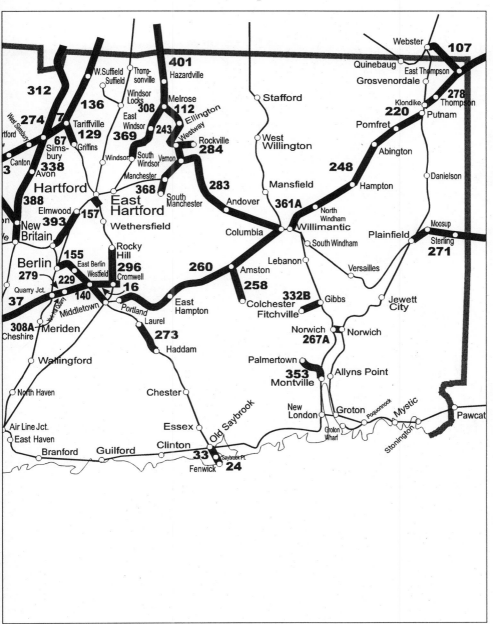

Connecticut

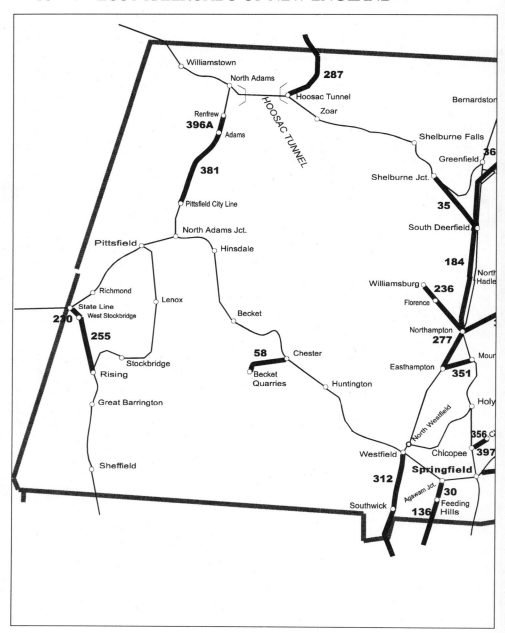

Western Massachusetts

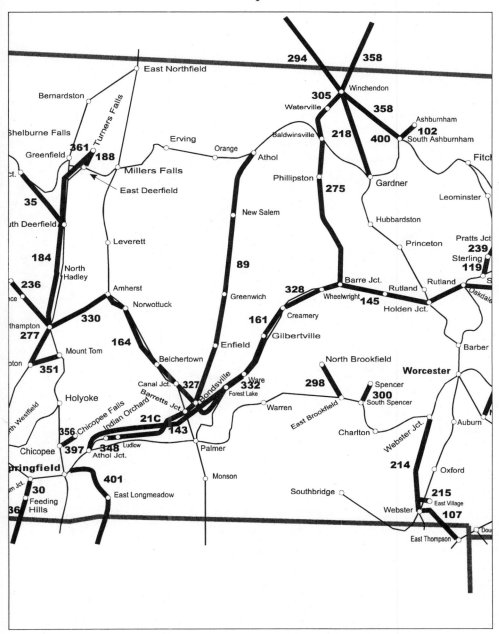

Western Massachusetts

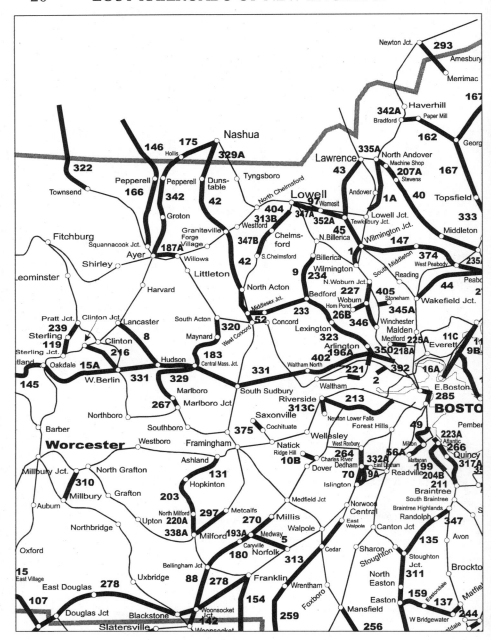

Eastern Massachusetts

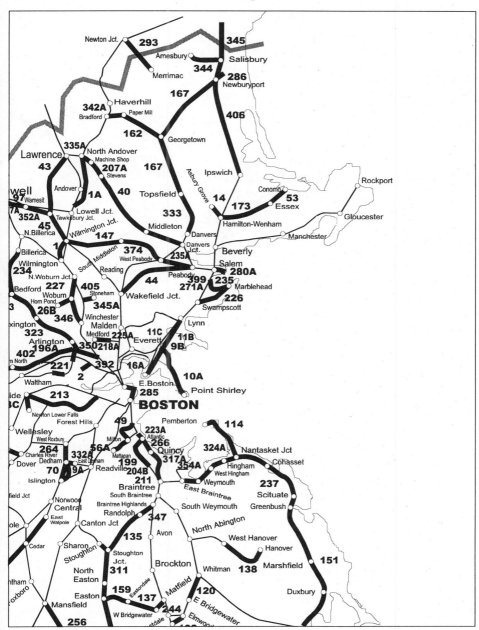

Eastern Massachusetts

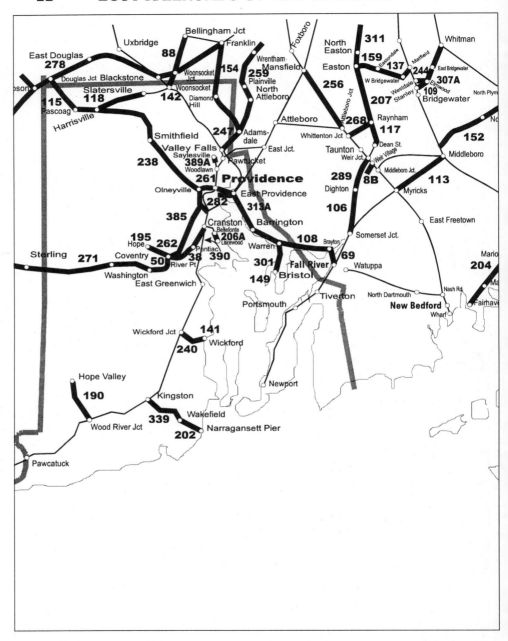

Rhode Island & Southeastern Massachusetts

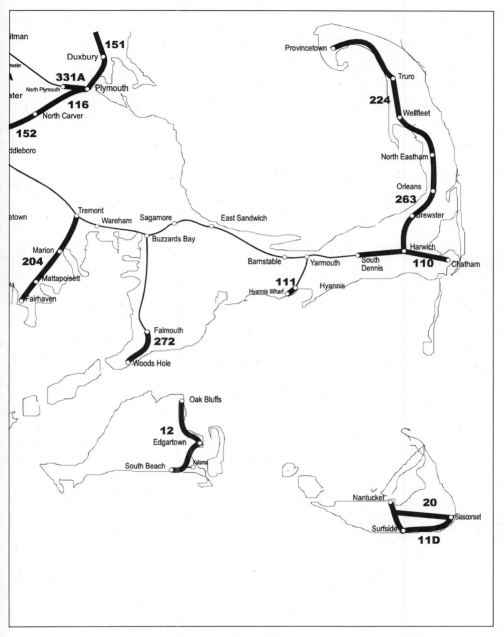

Rhode Island & Southeastern Massachusetts

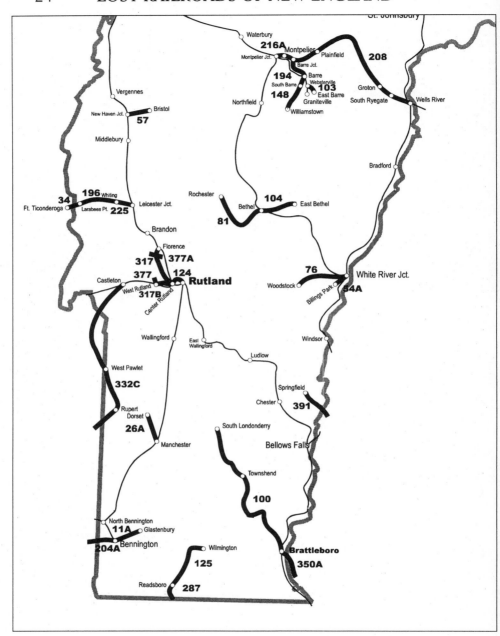

Vermont

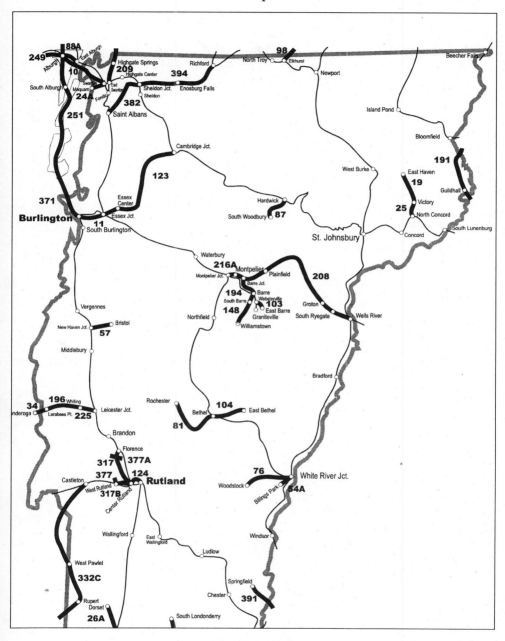

Vermont

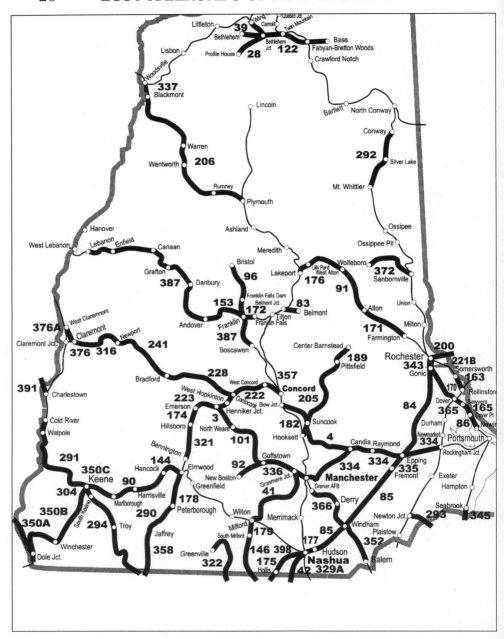

New Hampshire

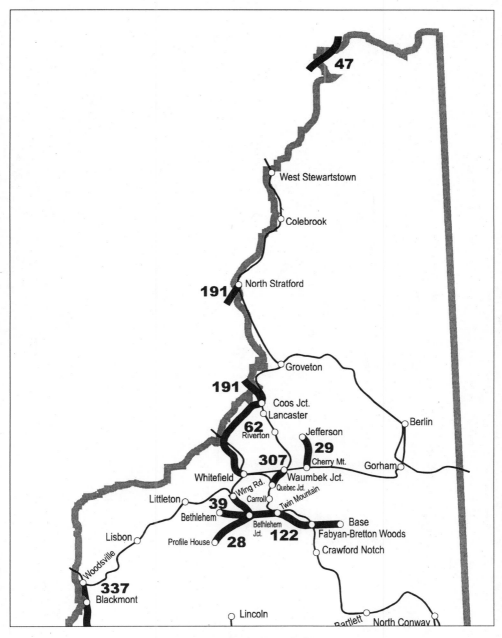

New Hampshire

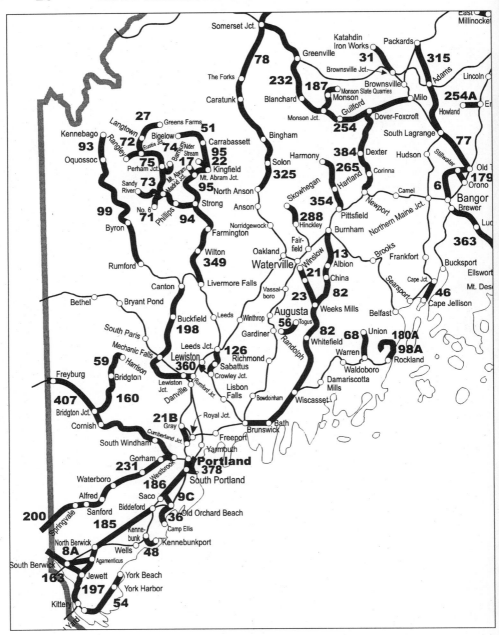

Southern Maine

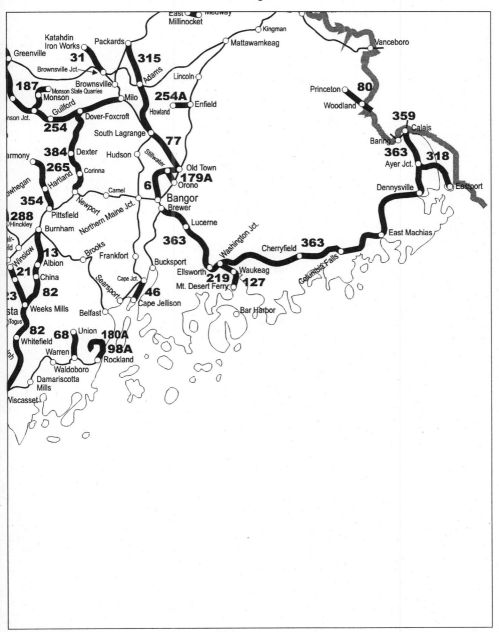

Southern Maine

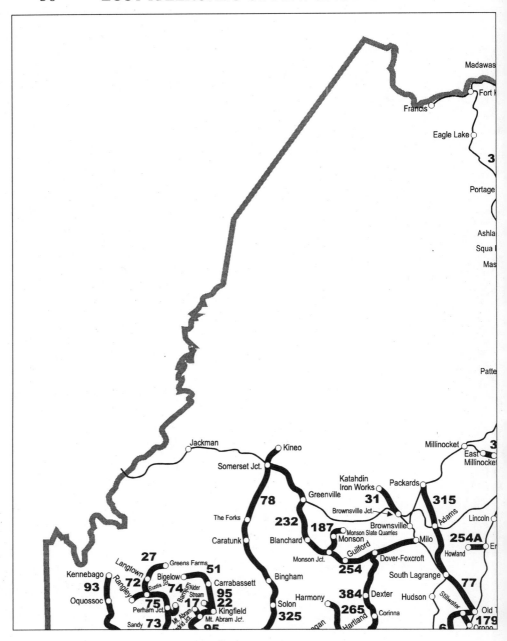

Northern Maine

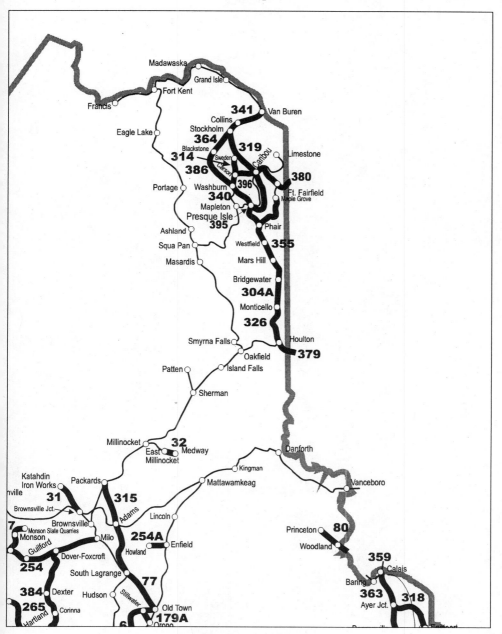

Northern Maine

1

The Rise and Fall of New England's Railroads

THE RAILROAD once tied New England together. In the early years of this century, when the region's rail network was at its peak, tracks crisscrossed the six New England states to reach virtually every city and town. Main lines connected major cities and branches served smaller settlements. Locomotives hauled in coal and cotton and took out manufactured goods for the rest of the nation. Passengers rode the coaches and sleepers that stopped at thousands of urban and rural depots.

Today, much of this system has vanished. Passengers, except for commuters, have largely deserted—or have been driven from—the rails, and most freight now travels by other modes. Few New Englanders burn coal in their homes, and what factories remain produce goods that reach their markets via highway or air. Some main lines continue, but much of the old rail network is now superfluous.

The railroad arrived too late in New England's history to have the effect it had on other regions, but this area can still boast a rich rail heritage. A primitive railroad was constructed on Boston's Beacon Hill as early as 1805. One of the earliest American railroads built according to a charter was the Granite Railway, which opened in 1826. This three-mile long pioneer railroad was constructed in Quincy, Massachusetts, to carry granite for the Bunker Hill Monument then under construction in Charlestown. Horses, not steam engines, hauled the stones from the quarries to the docks.

Two years after this photo was taken in 1974, fire destroyed the covered railroad bridge in Goffstown, N.H. The line was abandoned in 1981 (see line 336).

Steam locomotives were introduced in England about the same time, and by the early 1830s they were in use on railroads in Pennsylvania, Maryland, New York, New Jersey, and South Carolina. New England's first common carrier railroads—that is, built to carry both freight and passengers—received their charters in 1830 and 1831, a trio of lines out of Boston: the Boston & Lowell, the Boston & Worcester, and the Boston & Providence. The Boston & Worcester claimed the honor of operating New England's first steam railroad when it placed the initial portion of its line from Boston to Newton into service in April 1834. All three roads, which connected their namesake cities, were completed in the summer of 1835. All have remained important rail routes ever since, with thousands of commuters continuing to ride them daily.

During the 1840s charters were issued for rail lines to connect virtually all of New England's cities. By 1850 the key elements in the region's rail network were in place. Oddly enough, one of the most important links was among the last to be constructed: heavy competition from Long Island Sound steamboats delayed completion of the New York & New Haven Railroad until 1849.

Construction of new rail lines continued in the 1850s and 1860s. Cities and towns bypassed by the pioneer railroads were now connected to the main routes via numerous branch lines. Entire new systems, such as the Boston & New York Central direct line through Connecticut, were started. Another source of much new construction was the growing rivalry among competing railroads. At first the various states had attempted to regulate competition through the granting of monopolies, but these had expired after twenty or thirty years. By 1860 competing companies were free to obtain charters to build railroads parallel to existing lines or to construct branches into a rival's territory.

A good example of the excesses that resulted from cutthroat competition can be seen in Essex County, Massachusetts. Away from the coast and the Merrimack Valley most of the county was thinly populated; yet Essex could boast one of the densest rail networks in the region. The intense rivalry between the Boston & Maine and Eastern Railroads was largely responsible. Both lines battled for the Boston to Portland through traffic and at the same time hoped to increase their short hauls. In order to gain access to the port city of Salem on the Eastern main line, the B&M built or took over branches from its own through line. In return, the Eastern built its own branch from Salem to the B&M. A third road, the Boston & Lowell, also built its own Salem extension. Similarly, the B&M and Boston & Lowell each constructed branches to serve Lawrence and Lowell, which were on each others' main lines.

THE BOSTON & WORCESTER RAILROAD.

By the 1870s many of the formerly independent short railroads of New England had been consolidated into fourteen larger systems: the Maine Central; the Vermont Central and Rutland in Vermont; the Northern and the Boston, Concord & Montreal in New Hampshire; the Boston & Lowell, Boston & Maine, Eastern, Fitchburg, Boston & Albany, Boston & Providence, and Old Colony in Massachusetts; and the New Haven and the New York & New England in Connecticut and Rhode Island. Although nearly every town of any size was now served by one or more railroads, this did not deter new construction. Investors could be found for virtually any railroad scheme. For example, the 1880s saw the construction of the quixotic Central Massachusetts from Boston to Northampton, paralleling the main lines of the Fitchburg and Boston & Albany railroads, but managing to bypass all cities and large towns. One ultimately successful new system, the Bangor & Aroostook, was built after 1890. New rail construction in New England persisted into the new century; a new line between Hartford and Springfield (the third!) was opened as late as 1904, and the Bangor & Aroostook was not completed until around 1910.

By the beginning of the present century, the fourteen rail systems of 1870 were consolidated into six that persisted largely unchanged until the 1960s: the Bangor & Aroostook, the Maine Central-Boston & Maine, the Central Vermont, the Rutland, the Boston & Albany (New York Central), and New Haven. These were prosperous times for the railroads, which enjoyed an almost total monopoly of medium and long distance passenger and freight traffic. (Even some of the remaining competition, such as the street railway and the steamboat, were controlled by railroads). Passenger trains reached nearly every corner of the region. The depot had displaced the town green as the center of New England towns.

The decline of New England's rail system was as rapid as its rise. Automobiles had appeared in New England even before 1900 and trucks were introduced before 1910, but poor roads, a lack of mechanical reliability, and high costs generally restricted their use to the wealthy and the adventuresome before the First World War. The railroads remained unscathed by motor competition until the 1920s. Then within a few short years the automobile broke the railroad's monopoly of passenger travel, while the motor truck carried off increasing amounts of freight. Faced with declining revenues and rising costs, the Boston & Maine and New Haven railroads sought to rid themselves of unprofitable branch lines.

In 1920 Congress gave the federal Interstate Commerce Commission authority over all common carrier rail abandonments or construction. Railroads wishing to abandon trackage had to petition the I.C.C. for permission. The I.C.C. would not grant authority to abandon until public opinion had been heard. Not infrequently, protests from shippers and government officials prompted the I.C.C. to deny abandonment requests.

Only a few abandonments had occurred before 1920, in spite of the large amount of duplicate trackage that blanketed the region. Consolidation had seen many former main lines eliminated, but local traffic from rural depots and resort hotels, factories, coal and lumber yards, gravel pits, and grain dealers along the tracks kept the lines in use. In the 1920s, however, the automobile and truck carried away growing amounts of this local traffic. Many of the routes proposed for abandonment in the 1920s were lines serving mountain or shore resorts, whose predominately passenger traffic proved especially vulnerable to automotive competition.

The Great Depression of the 1930s accelerated the number of abandonments. By 1929 the automobile had already dealt a sharp blow to local rail passenger traffic. The railroads had countered by reducing or totally eliminating passenger service on many branches. After 1930, numerous factories closed, many permanently. With no passenger traffic and only an occasional carload of freight, trains became infrequent on many a branch line. Grass grew tall between the tracks, ties rotted, and rails rusted. The region's two largest railroads, the B&M and the New Haven, were bankrupt. The outlook for New England's railroads, as for New England itself, had never seemed bleaker.

War restored limited prosperity. After 1942 traffic increased significantly and abandonments largely ceased. Even though few of New England's shuttered mills reopened, the general postwar prosperity buoyed the fortunes of the railroads. New England railroads spent millions of dollars converting from steam to diesel power, and millions more went for new passenger and freight rolling stock. Few segments of track were let go during the late 1940s or the 1950s.

But national prosperity was not enough to sustain railroading in New England. Passengers continued to desert the rails in favor of automobiles and buses, and after the introduction of commercial jet service, increasing numbers took to the air. The construction of thousands of miles of limited access tollways and freeways directly subsidized the railroads' competition. Coal traffic dwindled as homes and factories converted to oil, natural gas, and electric heat and power. And the new high technology factories that opened or expanded in the 1960s, like Raytheon or Digital Equipment, had little use for rail service.

The most recent phase of New England's rail history began with the third and final bankruptcy of the New Haven Railroad in 1962. Wholesale abandonment of lightly used branches was sought as a means of stemming the railroad's losses. The region's weakest large railroad, the Rutland, had suspended operations in 1961 in the wake of a strike; the railroad was liquidated and abandoned in 1962. The railroad map of New England changed further in 1968, when the Boston & Albany (since 1960 an integral part of the New York Central, which had long controlled it) was absorbed into the new Penn Central Railroad. Federal regulators, under pressure from local

Boston & Maine 4-4-0, #33, the "Hercules," built by Hinckley in 1861, stops at Amesbury at the end of the now-abandoned Amesbury Branch in 1887 (see line 344). (Photo courtesy Walker Transportation Collection, Beverly Historical Society & Museum.)

officials, forced the PC to absorb the hapless New Haven in 1969. The following year the Penn Central itself crashed, the largest railroad failure in U.S. history. The Boston & Maine joined it in insolvency the same year.

By the early 1970s, with nearly all New England railroads at or approaching bankruptcy, it seemed that government ownership was the only alternative to the collapse of the entire system. Amtrak, Conrail, Metro North, and the state governments of Connecticut and Massachusetts did ultimately take over most of the old New Haven, and portions of the B&M and Boston & Albany to boot. But in a surprising development, Pittsburgh tycoon Timothy Mellon, heir to one of America's great fortunes, purchased control of the ailing B&M, Maine Central, and Delaware & Hudson railroads. He consolidated them under the banner of his Guilford Transportation Industries, and invested millions of his personal funds. His motives have never been entirely clear, but the result was a dramatic improvement in New England's rail climate. Guilford even absorbed some of the New Haven system in Connecticut that Conrail no longer wanted. Conrail itself surprised nearly everyone by becoming profitable. By the mid-1980s New England's railroads were healthier than they had been in decades.

These gains were made possible through changes in traditional railroad practices. Guilford clashed repeatedly with operating unions as it sought to increase profits by altering long-standing work rules to its advantage. Both Guilford and Conrail eliminated the caboose. Branch lines were a primary casualty of this modernization drive. Conrail and Guilford both viewed the high-density main line as the key to success; neither has much use for low-volume, labor-intensive branches. During the late 1970s and early 1980s, the number of rail abandonments increased anew. Many branch lines survive only with state subsidies, which can be withdrawn on short notice. Other lines, awaiting formal abandonment, have not seen trains in years. As the box car drifts into obsolescence the amount of surplus trackage in New England seems certain to increase. New England railroads are stronger today than anyone would have predicted twenty years ago, but the future promises many more abandonments.

2

The Saga of Lost Railroads

F ROM THE HILLS of Connecticut to the woods of Maine the ghostly paths of ancient railroads cross the New England landscape. Since 1848 more than 400 separate abandonments have occurred. Major rail systems have almost completely vanished. These include the New York & New England, the Central New England, the Worcester, Nashua & Portland, the Massachusetts Central, the Rutland, and the two-foot gauge systems of Maine. Most of these lines were always of marginal importance; the coming of the automobile and the motor carrier quickly rendered them obsolete. They now are gone, but they left their imprint on the New England landscape.

NOTE: Numbers in brackets refer to abandonments in chapter 4 and on the maps.

New York & New England

Since early New England railroads were built to link cities, a connection between Hartford and Providence seemed an obvious goal. In 1846 Providence businessmen launched the Providence & Plainfield Railroad west from their city toward Connecticut's capital. A Connecticut line, the Hartford, Providence & Fishkill, was chartered to continue the rails to Hartford, with hopes of ultimately reaching Waterbury or even the Hudson.

These ghostly stone pillars are all that remain of what once was an impressive steel bridge in Greenville, N.H. (see line 322).

These promoters were the first of many to underestimate the difficulty of crossing southern New England from east to west. Major streams in Connecticut, without exception, flow from north to south. River valleys thus make northward or southward travel easy; east-west routes encounter steep grades. Providence and Hartford are only sixty-five miles apart by air, but the surprisingly rugged topography of eastern Connecticut forced the new railroad to survey a twisting path fully ninety miles in length.

Construction of the Hartford, Providence & Fishkill (as the combined companies were henceforth known) began in 1847. Building proceeded simultaneously in two directions from Hartford: eastward toward Providence and westward toward Waterbury. Rails reached east to Willimantic and Plainfield in 1849 and west to Bristol the following year. Here the fledgling railroad ran out of cash. After intense lobbying, the municipal coffers of Hartford and Providence were tapped, and these funds enabled the HP&F to be completed to Providence in 1854 and Waterbury in 1855.

The new railroad quickly proved unprofitable, and bankruptcy followed in the wake of the financial panic of 1857. It was reorganized in 1863 as the Boston, Hartford & Erie, a name soon "synonymous with bankruptcy, litigation, fraud, and failure," in the words of Charles Francis Adams. Although the new railroad had inherited title to the Hartford, Providence & Fishkill, that line's bondholders continued to operate the railroad until 1878. Unable to gain control of the Providence-Hartford route, the promoters of the BH&E sought other lines. Their first acquisition was the Boston & New York Central, whose precarious condition belied its ambitious name.

The Boston & New York Central originated in 1846 when the Walpole Railroad was chartered to connect Walpole and Dedham, Massachusetts. A second railroad, the Norfolk County Railroad, chartered the following year, absorbed the first line and extended it southward. The Norfolk County opened between Dedham and Blackstone in 1849, and that same year the Southbridge & Blackstone was granted a charter to extend the rails westward. In 1850 the Midland Railroad was created to connect Dedham with Boston via Readville and Dorchester. Before these lines were completed they were consolidated to form the Boston & New York Central, a name that revealed the ultimate objective of its promoters. The new railroad was opened to Putnam, Connecticut, in 1854, and extended into Boston the year following.

Despite its pretentious title the B&NYC was a decrepit railroad. Traffic was scarce, and for several years in the late 1850s and early 1860s it does not appear to have been operated at all. The rails ended at Putnam, with no money to extend them toward New York. The road was reorganized several times before the newly formed Boston, Hartford & Erie acquired it in 1863. The BH&E at that time also took control of another small system of rail lines, the Charles River Railroad, that linked Boston (actually, Brookline) with Woonsocket, Rhode Island. The Charles River system intersected the B&NYC near Blackstone to form a large cross. The BH&E finally, in 1872, extended the old B&NYC from Putnam to Willimantic, where it met the Hartford, Providence & Fishkill.

As the BH&E closed in on Willimantic from the Northeast, another line was approaching it from the opposite direction. The New Haven, Middletown & Willimantic Railroad had been chartered in 1867 to connect its namesake cities, and with the help of local governments the line opened from New Haven to Middletown, on the Connecticut River, in 1870. Three years later it was finished to Willimantic, completing the long-sought direct inland route between Boston and New York via the BH&Eand the New Haven. But the promised traffic never materialized; the New Haven, Middletown & Willimantic soon was in receivership. Reorganization followed, with the company emerging as the Boston & New York Air-Line Railroad. The Air-Line entered into a pooling agreement with the New Haven in 1879 and was leased by that system in 1882.

In 1873 the ramshackle BH&E—an assemblage of marginal railroads—was reorganized as the New York & New England Railroad, "the strangest, most loose-jointed, shambling, anomalous congeries of rails, with the most melodious name in all the six states," to quote rail historian Alvin Harlow. Legal complications prvented the NY&NE from taking contol of the BH& E for two years. In 1881 the NY&NE completed the long-awaited extension of ts rails from Waterbury through Danbury to Brewster, New York. The NY&NE also absorbed several shorter Connecticut railroads at this time.

During the 1880s and early 1890s the NY&NE battled the New Haven for the railroad traffic of southern New England. Despite the intensity of this rivalry, the two systems cooperated in operating a crack express train. In 1884 the New England Limited began operating between Boston and New York in a mere six hours, via the old Boston & New York Central route of the NY&NE between Boston and Willimantic and thence over the New Haven's Air-Line from Willimantic to New Haven and the New Haven's main line to New York city. The New England Limited stopped only in Willimantic, Middletown, New Haven, and Bridgeport. In 1891 the entire train, cars and locomotives, was painted white, and the Limited quickly acquired the enduring nickname of White Train or Ghost Train. Popular with passengers but difficult to keep clean, the train was discontinued in 1895. Its replacement, the Air Line Limited, made the passage between Boston and New York in a record five hours and forty minutes, with a single stop at Willimantic to change engines.

The NY&NE was at a severe disadvantage in its competition with the mighty New Haven. Its main lines were plagued with steep grades and sharp curves, its treasury was chronically underfunded, and the thinly populated territory it traversed generated light traffic. The New Haven gained a decisive edge in 1889 when the final bridge was completed on its shore line route, giving it a superior all-rail route between Boston and New York. The NY&NE managed to hold on until 1895 when the New Haven finally gained control. Under the New Haven the old Boston & New York Central, Hartford, Providence & Fishkill, and the Air-Line were kept intact, although trains

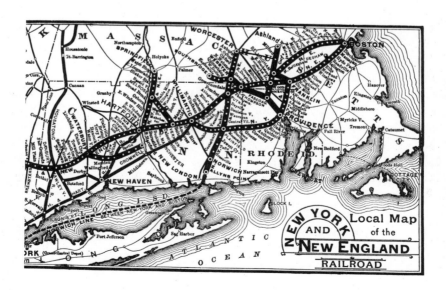

ran less frequently. Through passenger service between Boston and New York via Willimantic ended in 1924, and all passenger service on the Air-Line was discontinued by 1937. By then passenger service on the Providence to Willimantic segment of the old Hartford, Providence & Fishkill had also ended.

Passenger trains continued to operate on the Boston-Willimantic-Hartford-Waterbury route for many years, until heavy flooding in August 1955 washed out a bridge near Putnam, Connecticut.The New Haven "temporarily" suspended passenger service on the Boston-Hartford route; it never was restored. Local passenger service between Hartford and Waterbury lasted until 1959, and commuter trains ran from Boston to Blackstone through 1966, when the route was cut back to Franklin.

Freight traffic also declined, but the system remained intact until the 1930s. A twelve-mile portion of the Brewster extension between Allerton Farms (just west of Waterbury) and Southbury, Connecticut, was abandoned in 1937 [105], and another nine miles from Southbury to Hawleyville was let go in 1948 [193]. The remainder of the NY&NE survived until 1959, when the I.C.C. approved abandonment of the four-mile segment of the old Boston & New York Central between Putnam and Pomfret, Connecticut, that had been out of service since the 1955 floods [220]. The inland route between Boston and New York was now permanently severed.

The bankruptcy of the New Haven in 1962 produced a wave of abandonments that swept away much of the NY&NE. First to go in 1963 were eighteen miles between Pomfret and North Windham[248]. Two years later the entire eastern section of the Air-Line, twenty-five miles from Portland (across the Connecticut River from Middletown) to Willimantic, was given up [258, 260]. Portions of these rights-of-way have subsequently been acquired by the State of Connecticut for use as hiking and bridle trails. Before the end of the decade two more key segments of the NY&NE vanished: eighteen miles of the Hartford, Providence & Fishkill between Coventry, Rhode Island, and Plainfield, Connecticut, in 1967 [271]; and thirty-two miles of the Boston & New York Central from Franklin, Massachusetts, to Putnam, Connecticut, two years later [278].

The most recent abandonment of the NY&NE took place in 1970, following the absorption of the New Haven into the Penn

Central Railroad. Another twenty miles of the Hartford, Providence & Fishkill between Manchester and Columbia (near Willimantic), Connecticut, were given up [283, 284]. Today, the remaining segments of the former main lines of the NY&NE are disconnected branches operated by Conrail, Guilford, the Providence & Worcester, and the MBTA. The route of the Ghost Train has itself become a phantom.

Central New England

At the end of the Civil War the citizens of Hartford and northeastern Connecticut were seized by the idea that their continued prosperity was dependent on acquiring a direct rail line from Hartford to the Hudson and the West. After all, Boston already enjoyed one such route (the Boston & Albany) and was building another (the Fitchburg). Unless Hartford took action, Springfield and New Haven would siphon off the remaining western traffic and leave Hartford high and dry. In 1868 promoters secured a charter for the Connecticut Western Railroad, to run west from Hartford along the Massachusetts border to the Hudson. Construction began shortly afterward, and the line was completed from Hartford through Winsted and Canaan to Millerton, New York, in 1871. At Millerton the CW connected with the newly constructed Dutchess & Columbia Railroad, which extended to the Hudson at Beacon. Soon an extension over a subsidiary gave the CW direct access to the Hudson at Rhinecliff.

Traffic on the CW, consisting primarily of Pennsylvania coal, fell short of expectations, and a major accident at Tariffville, Connecticut, in 1878, in which thirteen people died, resulted in heavy legal expenses. The CW slid into bankruptcy in 1880 and was reorganized as the Hartford & Connecticut Western. In 1889 the entire railroad, both in Connecticut and New York, was absorbed by the Central New England & Western Railroad.

The CNE&W was controlled by the owners of the new 6600-foot rail bridge across the Hudson at Poughkeepsie, New York. The CW had been acquired to feed traffic over that route. Using the route of the CW, increased carloads of Pennsylvania coal entered New England. Even a few through passenger trains now traveled the CW, including the Boston-to-Harrisburg Day Express and the Boston-to-Washington, D.C., Federal.

In 1892 Pennsylvania coal baron A. A. McLeod, who controlled the Philadelphia & Reading Railroad, took charge of the CNE&W, merged it with the Poughkeepsie Bridge and its western approaches, and rechristened the new system the Philadelphia, Reading & New England Railroad. Shortly afterwards McLeod bought control of the New York & New England and the B&M. But the audacious McLeod soon met his match in the mighty New Haven and its kingpin, the all-powerful J. P. Morgan. Defiant, McLeod proclaimed that he would rather run a peanut stand than be dictated to by Morgan; Morgan responded by crushing the upstart Pennsylvanian with no more apparent effort than it would have taken to flick an ash from his cigar. By the end of 1893 McLeod's rail empire was in ruins, and the Philadelphia, Reading & New England was on its own.

The PR&NE was reorganized in 1899 to form the Central New England Railway. The new railroad company was one of only two remaining railroads of any size in southern New England not under

General View of the Poughkeepsie Bridge.

the control of the New Haven. Virtually its only asset was its magnificent bridge over the Hudson at Poughkeepsie. Before it bowed to the inevitable and surrendered its independence, the CNE made one last effort to remain viable. It began construction of a fourteen-mile extension from its main line at Tariffville, Connecticut, to the main line of the Boston & Albany at Agawam Junction, just west of Springfield. Trackage rights were obtained from the B&A that would bring the CNE into Springfield proper, where it would interchange with the B&M. But just as the new line was set to open in 1900, a New Haven Railroad crew ripped up 200 feet of CNE track, and the New Haven secured a court injunction that forbade reinstallation. The New Haven's lawyers prevented the branch's opening until 1904.

In 1903 the New Haven secured nearly total monopoly over the rails of southern New England when it acquired the CNE, primarily to obtain the Poughkeepsie Bridge. Partly as a concession to strong anti-monopoly sentiment, the CNE retained its identity and was operated separately from the rest of the New Haven system. Aside from its bridge, however, the CNE had little to contribute to its new owners. Practically every town of any consequence on the CNE was already served by an existing New Haven line. Under New Haven control, passenger trains on the CNE dwindled, and freight traffic (nearly all of which was coal) remained modest. Steep grades on the New York portions of the CNE discouraged through traffic, and the sparsely populated territory through which the railroad passed contributed little local traffic.

The CNE remained intact until 1921, when the railroad received permission to abandon a portion of its Springfield branch between the connection with the B&A at Agawam Junction and Feeding Hills, Massachusetts. The tracks remained in place, however, until 1938 [30]. Passenger service on the remainder of the CNE ended in December 1927. The system somehow stumbled on until the 1930s, when the Great Depression finally forced the New Haven to throw in the towel. In 1932 the connection between the old CW main line and the Poughkeepsie bridge was severed, rendering the CNE a long branch to nowhere. Without through traffic, the isolated Connecticut towns along the CNE could not sustain the railroad. Later that same year, service was suspended on key segments of the CNE, fragmenting the railroad into a series of short New Haven branch lines. Formal abandonment of the system began in 1937, and most of the system was gone by the end of 1940. [63-67, 129-30, 132, 136, 156].

Today, nearly the entire route of the CNE is a ghost railroad. Ten miles of former CNE trackage from Canaan to Lakeville, Connecticut, continued to be operated as a New Haven branch until 1965 [257], and a short stretch of the former Springfield branch at Simsbury, Connecticut, was in use until 1968 [274]. Aside from isolated short segments used as yard or industrial trackage, the only significant portion of the CNE remaining in service is the initial eight miles of the old railroad, from Hartford to Griffins, Connecticut. In the early 1970s, freight traffic on this branch of the Penn Central was so slight that the federal government proposed that it be excluded from the new Conrail system. Vigorous local and state objections reversed the recommendation. In 1982 the B&M took over operation of the branch from Conrail but discontinued operation soon afterwards. Recently, the line was upgraded and was slated to be back in service in 1996.

Worcester, Nashua & Rochester

Worcester is one of the few cities in New England whose growth is clearly linked to the railroad. In 1835, when the Boston & Worcester Railroad arrived, the town of Worcester numbered about 5,000 inhabitants. By 1850, the new city of Worcester contained 17,000; by 1870, some 41,000; and by 1900, nearly 120,000. Worcester was the terminus of the Western Railroad to Springfield, Albany, and the West (1841); the Norwich & Worcester, to the steamboats on Long Island Sound (1840); and the Providence & Worcester (chartered 1844, completed 1847, along the route of the old Blackstone Canal).

With railroads fanning out from Worcester in many directions, it was not surprising that by the mid-1840s serious thought was given to a northeast line toward the bustling textile mills of the Merrimack Valley and perhaps beyond to Maine and the Maritimes. The Worcester & Nashua was duly chartered by Massachusetts in 1845 to build from Worcester to the New Hampshire border; another railroad had already been chartered in New Hampshire the previous year to bring the rails into Nashua. The two companies were merged in 1846 under the name of the Massachusetts company. Construction of the Massachusetts portion of the line began in 1846, and the railroad was opened in its entirety, by way of Groton Junction (now Ayer), where it met the recently completed Fitchburg Railroad, to Nashua in December 1848. During its early years the Worcester & Nashua was fairly prosperous. Considerable passenger and freight traffic entered and left the railroad at Worcester and Nashua; at Groton Junction (where the Stony Brook branch of the Nashua & Lowell provided access to Lowell and Lawrence); and at Sterling Junction (where the Fitchburg & Worcester Railroad connected).

Meanwhile, a second railroad was taking shape 150 miles to the northeast. In 1846 backers of the York & Cumberland Railroad had received a charter to construct a line from Portland southwest to South Berwick, Maine. Construction did not start until 1850. By 1853 the rails had reached the Saco River, a mere 18 miles out of Portland. Here the line stopped, "bogged down," as Alvin Harlow put it. The short railroad ended at the Saco for more than a decade. After the Civil War, a new group of owners with ambitious plans took charge of the York & Cumberland. Extensions were projected to Nashua, the Hoosac Tunnel, or even Boston, by way of Rochester, New Hampshire, the up-and-coming rail crossroads of northern New England. The York & Cumberland was rechristened the Portland & Rochester, and the city of Portland was persuaded to kick in $700,000 to aid in the construction of thirty-four miles to Rochester. In 1871 the P&R, in John Kirkland's words, "staggered into Rochester," and promptly obtained still more aid from Portland. Unfortunately, the connection at Rochester to the south did not materialize, and the weak railroad barely survived the depression that began in 1873.

The Worcester & Nashua had looked on with great interest at these developments to the north. The prospect of opening its own line to Portland was too alluring to pass up. The Worcester & Nashua obtained a charter for an extension, the Nashua & Rochester, and the new line was completed to Rochester in November 1874. Nine years later the Worcester & Nashua and Nashua & Rochester railroads were consolidated to form the Worcester, Nashua & Rochester Railroad. The extension to Rochester proved to be a costly mistake for the hitherto prosperous Worcester & Nashua. Heavily in debt from construction costs, the railroad almost failed in the crash of 1873.

FOSTER STREET STATION FROM THE EAST.
FROM BRADBURY AND GUILD'S RAILROAD CHART, 1847.

The inland Worcester-Nashua-Rochester-Portland route was simply not competitive with the older coastal routes from southern New England.

The Portland & Rochester was in an especially sorry state. Most of its stocks and bonds were owned by the city of Portland until 1877, when the city unloaded its holdings at a fraction of their original cost. Two years later the Eastern Railroad, its rival to the east, obtained control; in 1884 the Eastern system itself was swallowed by the Boston & Maine. To the south, the Worcester, Nashua & Rochester maintained its independence until 1886 when it too was absorbed by the B&M. For the first time the entire Worcester-to-Portland route was under a single management.

The Portland & Rochester and the Worcester, Nashua & Rochester together now formed the Worcester, Nashua & Portland division of the B&M. Two through passenger trains plied the entire route in 1893, covering the 147-mile journey in five and a half hours. Most of the traffic over the route, however, was confined to the southernmost sector, the old Worcester & Nashua. A total of thirteen daily passenger trains were scheduled between Worcester and Nashua in 1893, compared to seven between Nashua and Rochester and six between Rochester and Portland.

By the early 1930s passenger service had been reduced to a pair of single daily gas-electric "doodlebug" cars, one between Worcester and Nashua and the other from Nashua to Portland, with an average passenger load of six. With an abundance of parallel routes, the B&M sent little through freight traffic over the division. In 1932 the B&M requested permission to abandon two large segments of the old Nashua & Rochester between Hudson and Fremont (21 miles) and between Epping and Gonic, New Hampshire (18 miles). Following objections from New Hampshire's Attorney General, the B&M changed its petition to a request for an abandonment of service only, leaving the tracks in place. All service ceased on these two segments March 5, 1934 [84, 85]. Passenger service north of Nashua ended at the same time. On April 15 passenger trains made their last runs between Ayer and Nashua. The state of New Hampshire, which now sought portions of the railroad right of way to use for a highway, withdrew its previous objection. The I.C.C. gave permission to abandon the two discontinued segments, and the tracks were removed.

Local freight traffic on the remaining portions of the WN&R was light. In 1941 the B&M petitioned four miles between Nashua and Hudson, New Hampshire [177] and eight miles between Nashua and Pepperell, Massachusetts [175]. Permission was granted for the first item, but objections from the state of New Hampshire and shippers persuaded the I.C.C. to grant only partial approval of the second. The first four miles out of Nashua to Hollis, New Hampshire, had been used for only one twelve-day-period since 1934, but the depot at Hollis still received shipments from the south. The I.C.C. gave its approval to abandon the Nashua-Hollis segment, but the rest of the line remained for another forty years.

In 1949 the B&M announced plans to ditch forty-six miles of the old Portland & Rochester, from Westbrook, Maine, (six miles out of Portland) to Rochester, New Hampshire. Samuel M. Pinsly, the short line baron of Boston, purchased the line from the B&M, and renamed it the Sanford & Eastern. The new short line was in trouble from the beginning. The westernmost sixteen miles of the S&E were abandoned in 1952 [200]. The rest of the railroad held on for another nine years until 1961, when the closing of the Goodall-Sanford mills, its primary shipper, forced the S&E to fold [231].

Three short remnants of the WN&R survived until recently. Three and a half miles of ex-Nashua & Rochester trackage between Epping and Fremont, New Hampshire, were abandoned in 1981 [335], and twelve miles of the former Worcester & Nashua from Ayer, Massachusetts, to Hollis, New Hampshire, met the same fate the following year [342]. By 1989 the state of Massachusetts had acquired the latter line for use as a recreational trail. The initial 1.6 miles of the line out of Nashua continued to be used to service a few Nashua customers until the late 1980s and was not abandoned until 1993 [398].

Aside from a short length of ex-Portland & Rochester trackage near Portland and very brief segments elsewhere, the only surviving portion of the entire Worcester, Nashua & Portland division is the initial twenty miles from Worcester to Ayer. This has always been the busiest section of the division, since it gives the B&M its only access to Worcester. Beyond Ayer, the road to Portland is a fading memory.

Massachusetts Central

Projecting, promoting, and constructing railroads was among the most exciting pursuits in nineteenth-century America. The railroad mania was apt to strike in the most unlikely places. Few if any spots in the United States could boast a denser rail network in the late 1860s than eastern and central Massachusetts; yet, even here, there were those who sought to build more. Two prosperous railroads, the Boston & Albany and the Fitchburg, operated busy main lines from Boston westward to the Connecticut River valley, no more than forty miles apart. Together they served every town of any substance in the region. (Wayland, the largest community without rail service, had less than 1800 inhabitants.) It would seem to have been sheer folly to build still a third line, one that would bypass all of the commercial and industrial centers served by the other two railroads. Folly or not, the third line came to be built.

In 1868 the Wayland & Sudbury Branch Railroad was authorized to construct a seven-mile line from Weston, on the main line of the Fitchburg, to Sudbury. Later that same year a citizens' meeting at

Barre called for the building of a Massachusetts Central Railroad from Boston to Northampton, including the new and as yet unbuilt Wayland & Sudbury. The legislature granted this request in 1869, chartering the Massachusetts Central to run from Weston to Northampton. The new railroad set about raising funds by selling its securities to the governments of towns along its route. Its chief asset, however, was the strong political support it enjoyed in the state legislature, probably as a result of the unpopularity of its rivals.

Surveying began almost immediately, and actual construction commenced in 1871, westward from Weston. An agreement was reached with the Boston & Lowell to use the latter's Boston terminal. The first of many disasters to plague this unfortunate line struck in 1873 when the contractor who was building the railroad failed. All work ceased for five years. In 1878 a new charter was secured authorizing the construction of a line from Weston to Boston, and construction resumed. In October 1881 the first twenty-eight miles from Boston to Hudson were opened, and by 1882 trains ran as far west as Jeffersons, forty-six miles from Boston.

The railroad's success was short lived. In May 1883 the ailing railroad once more ran out of cash. Operations were suspended for more than two years. The Massachusetts Central was then reorganized as the Central Massachusetts Railroad, and operation was taken over by the Boston & Lowell. In September 1885 trains ran once more. The Boston & Lowell formally leased the Central Massachusetts in 1886; the following year the B&L itself was absorbed, along with the Central Massachusetts, by the Boston & Maine. Again construction resumed, and in December 1887 the line finally was completed to Northampton. It had taken more than sixteen years to build a hundred-mile railroad.

The first years under B&M auspices were the glory days of the Central Mass. The B&M used the line to compete with the Boston & Albany and the Fitchburg for through traffic from the West. Passenger trains from points as distant as Harrisburg, Pennsylvania, and Washington, D.C., used the Central Mass to reach Boston by way of the Poughkeepsie Bridge, the Connecticut Western, and the New Haven railroads. Long-distance passenger service ended abruptly in November 1893 with the collapse of A.A. McLeod's rail empire (see the above section on the Connecticut Western). And after the B&M absorbed its last Massachusetts rival, the Fitchburg, in 1900, the

Central Mass was of marginal worth for either passenger or freight traffic.

The first abandonment on the Central Mass occurred in 1903 when construction of the Wachusett Reservoir flooded out seven miles of track between West Berlin and Oakdale [15A]. Rather than replace these tracks, the B&M rerouted Central Mass traffic over a parallel section of the Worcester, Nashua & Portland division. Four miles of new track were built to provide the necessary connections, including a viaduct and a tunnel at Clinton.

Through passenger service between Boston and Northampton over the Central Mass declined from three to two daily round trips during the 1920s. On April 23, 1932, all passenger service west of Clinton ceased. Freight traffic also declined. In order to reduce losses, the B&M in 1931 and 1932 obtained trackage rights over sections of the Central Vermont and the Winchendon Branch of the B&A that paralleled the Central Mass. Connections were constructed, and service on the Central Mass lines ended.

The torrential rains that accompanied the hurricane of September 1938 brought severe flooding to much of New England, including the right of way of the Central Mass. Even before the floods, freight service had been discontinued between Oakdale and Rutland. Trackage at New Barre Plains was washed away and not repaired. In 1939 the I.C.C. authorized the B&M to abandon twenty-four miles of the Central Mass between Oakdale and Wheelwright [145]. The Central Mass had been severed to form two long branches, from Northampton eastward to Wheelwright and from Boston west to Oakdale.

Passenger service continued on the eastern segment of the Central Mass from Boston to Clinton. The last regularly scheduled steam locomotives on the B&M plied this route daily until replaced by diesels in 1956. As of August 11, 1958, passenger trains terminated at Hudson and freight service was cut back to Boston-Berlin. The trackage between Clinton and Berlin was abandoned [216]. On January 15, 1965, South Sudbury became the terminus of passenger service. A single daily Budd RDC car provided service over the route under the auspices of the MBTA until 1971, when the number of trains was increased to four daily round trips. On November 26, 1971, however, all passenger service ended.

The two branches that had once formed the Central Mass retained some freight traffic into the 1970s. In 1980, however, the B&M effectively abandoned the remainder of the Central Mass. The entire western segment, from Northampton east to Wheelwright—forty miles of track and trackage rights—was given up [328, 330, 332]. At the same time the eastern part from Berlin to Waltham North went to the wreckers [331]. The last remnant of the Central Mass, a mile and half of track between Waltham North and Clematis Brook, was abandoned in 1994 [402]. A hundred-mile railroad had become a memory. (This section relies heavily on the excellent history *The Central Mass.*, Boston & Maine Railroad Historical Society, Inc., 1975).

Rutland

Abandoned railroads do not always stay abandoned. More than one New England line has arisen phoenix-like to a second life. In fact, at least two segments of track have been abandoned, rebuilt, and then abandoned a second time [3 and 101; 9 and 234]. The most spectacular return from oblivion was the restoration of much of the old Rutland Railroad, whose collapse was the largest single abandonment in New England history.

The Rutland system traced its origins to 1843 with the chartering of the Champlain & Connecticut River Railroad, which received permission to build a line from Burlington, Vermont, to the Connecticut River valley. The line was supposed to prosper by hauling the heavy "Lakes to Boston" traffic that would presumably flow from Canada and the West into New England—traffic that never lived up to expectations. The day before the C&C received its charter, the Vermont legislature had created another railroad, the Vermont Central, with authority to build over a roughly parallel route. The struggle between these two railroads dominated the railroad history of the Green Mountain State for the next half century.

The C&CR became the Rutland & Burlington in 1847, and construction commenced the same year at Bellows Falls on the Connecticut. The line was opened between Bellows Falls and Chester in the summer of 1849 and was completed to Burlington by the end of the year. Meanwhile, the rival Vermont Central was one step ahead, beating the Rutland & Burlington by several months for the honor of operating the first railroad in Vermont, and then completing its own line first to Burlington through White River Junction and Montpelier.

The heated competition between the two railroads was fought both in the field and in the legislature. The anticipated traffic from the West never materialized, leaving two companies to scrap over business scarcely adequate for one. Both railroads stepped in and out of bankruptcy in the 1850s and 1860s. In 1867 the Rutland & Burlington was reorganized as the Rutland Railroad. Three years later the Vermont Central leased the Rutland and consolidated its rival, but this could not save it from failure. The expanded Vermont Central folded after the panic of 1873, and was then reorganized as the Central Vermont. It operated in receivership for another eleven years.

The Rutland remained an integral part of the Central Vermont until 1896, when it regained its independence. In 1899 it built an extension over Lake Champlain to Rouses Point, New York, which gave it a direct route to Canada and the West. The year following, it leased the Bennington & Rutland Railroad, which gave it access to New York state. The Bennington & Rutland, which had been chartered as the Western Vermont Railroad in 1845, opened in 1852 and subsequently passed through various ownerships (including the Central Vermont between 1873 and 1877). In the early 1870s promoters had tried to make it part of a new New York City-Montreal route.

By the 1890s the route had materialized, with through sleepers from New York City traveling via the New York Central to Troy, New York; the Fitchburg to Bennington; and the Bennington & Rutland, the Rutland, and the Central Vermont to Canada.

In the early twentieth century, the Rutland came under the control of the New York Central, although the line was run independently. Two daily New York-to-Montreal passenger trains, the Green Mountain Flyer and the Mount Royal, were operated for many years, with connecting sections from Boston via the Boston & Maine. But as with most railroads, it was freight that paid the bills; and the picturesque Vermont countryside produced little traffic. Bankrupt in 1938, the Rutland was not reorganized until 1950. By mid-century nearly all of its equipment were relics. Passenger service ended in 1953 when a strike by Rutland employees gave management an opportunity to halt this costly operation.

For a time in the mid-1950s, the Rutland seemed to get back on its feet, with new diesel locomotives and freight cars, and the elimination of the passenger deficit. But the losses soon returned. The refusal of Rutland management to follow the 1960 National Rail Wage Agreement brought on another strike by Rutland employees. On September 25, 1961, the railroad suspended all operations. The Rutland never ran again. The owners of the Rutland petitioned the I.C.C. to abandon the entire railroad. After a long series of hearings and appeals, on September 18, 1962, the I.C.C. approved the abandonment (effective early 1963), and the Rutland was no more. A total of 332 miles of lines in Vermont and New York were given up, by far the largest single abandonment in New England rail history.

In 1963 the state of Vermont purchased 180 miles of former Rutland trackage south of Burlington. Two new privately-owned railroads were organized to operate the state's trackage. The Vermont Railway, 124 miles between Burlington and Bennington, came into operation in January 1964. The tracks of the new railroad had been formally abandoned for a year and had been out of service for more than two. Another fifty-two miles of Rutland trackage between Rutland and Bellows Falls was brought back into service in April 1965 by the Green Mountain Railroad. For many years steam passenger excursions were operated over parts of this line in conjunction with the Steamtown USA rail museum at Bellows Falls, until the museum moved to Pennsylvania.

Today much of the Rutland is a living ghost. While the New York & New England, the Central Mass, and the Worcester, Nashua & Portland are gone and mostly forgotten, under other names the Rutland lives on.

The Two-Footers

Until recently, thousands of visitors traveled each year to South Carver, Massachusetts, to visit the Edaville Railroad. This popular operating museum preserved the last vestiges of a unique institution, the very narrow gauge railway. The diminutive engines and rolling stock of the Edaville once plied the deep woods of Maine, over several rail systems now totally abandoned.

More than a century ago, American railroads adopted a standard gauge of four feet, eight and a half inches between the rails. In the early days of railroading a variety of gauges were in use, making it impossible for rolling stock to travel over different lines. Some gauges were narrow, while others, including the six-foot gauge of the Erie Railroad, and the five-and-a-half-foot roads of Maine, were wide. It was not until after the Civil War, however, that it became fashionable to build narrow gauge lines. Narrow gauge railroads, it was argued, would be cheaper to construct, maintain, and operate, especially in mountainous terrain. By the end of the 1870s, several dozen narrow gauge rail systems were in operation, under construction, or projected, primarily in the western states.

Most of the new narrow gauge systems settled on a gauge of three feet. A few contended that even smaller gauges should be built. In 1875 one George E. Mansfield, of Hazelhurst, Massachusetts, learned that the citizens of Billerica were seeking a branch line to serve their town. Mansfield passionately believed that two-foot gauge railroads were the wave of the future. He had already constructed a short experimental two-foot gauge railroad near his house, along the lines of a two-foot line he had actually ridden in Wales. Rushing to Billerica, Mansfield persuaded the local inhabitants to adopt his hitherto untried scheme. In May 1877 the Billerica & Bedford

Railroad received its charter as the nation's first two-foot gauge common carrier railroad. Mansfield was named general manager.

Despite financial support from local governments and residents, the fledgling line was chronically short of cash. The road was con-

structed, as cheaply as possible, from North Billerica station on the Boston & Lowell 8.6 miles to Bedford. The line was completed in November 1877. Within two months the Billerica & Bedford was in receivership, and in June 1878 all operations ceased. With little fanfare the line was quickly dismantled [9]. In 1886 the Boston & Lowell rebuilt the line as a standard gauge branch line. The B&L's successor, the B&M, abandoned it in 1962 [234].

During its brief period of operation the B&B attracted numerous observers, including a few from Maine. Some of these northern visitors invited George Mansfield to come and describe the advantages of two-foot gauge railroads. Mansfield, happy to oblige, ventured north to Franklin County, Maine, in March 1878, preaching the two-foot gospel to the citizens of Rangley, Strong, Phillips, and Madrid. When the B&B collapsed, it had in its possession two new Forney-type locomotives and several passenger, freight, and work cars. Mansfield persuaded a group of Franklin County businessmen to organize the Sandy River Railroad and to acquire this rolling stock.

The new railroad, the first of the Maine two-footers, was chartered in March 1879, and construction began shortly afterwards from Farmington on the Maine Central. The first eighteen miles to Phillips opened on November 20, 1879. Unlike its Massachusetts predecessor, however, the Sandy River was a success. Its relative prosperity produced imitation and expansion. The Franklin & Megantic Railroad was chartered in 1883 from Strong on the Sandy River fifteen miles to Kingfield. Construction began the following year and the line was soon completed. Plagued by 5-percent grades, rough track, and heavy winter snows, the F&M was less successful than the Sandy River. In 1894 a third two-footer, the Kingfield & Dead River Railroad, extended the route another nine miles to Carrabasset; a final six-mile extension to Bigelow was finished in 1900.

Meanwhile, the Phillips & Rangeley Railroad had been chartered in 1889 to form another extension of the Sandy River line, twenty-eight miles from Phillips on the Sandy River to Rangeley. The P&R was built to exploit a large stand of virgin spruce and also to serve resorts at Rangeley. The line was opened to its terminus at the Marbles Hotel, just beyond Rangeley, in July 1891. The new railroad was moderately successful, not as profitable as the Sandy River, but better than the hapless Franklin & Megantic.

The Phillips & Rangley, Franklin & Megantic, Kingfield & Dead River, and Sandy River were brought together in 1908 to form the Sandy River & Rangley Lake Railroad, a 101-mile two-foot railroad system. The combined company enjoyed several profitable years of operation, until the Maine Central obtained control in 1911. Three branches were abandoned as lumbering declined: the two-mile branch to Mt. Abram in 1905 [17]; another two-mile line to Alder Stream in 1916 [22]; and four miles to Langtown in 1919 [27]. World War I brought brisk business to the SR&RL, pulpwood accounting for most of the traffic. But after the war's end, declining revenues and mounting debts quickly overwhelmed the small railroad. Bankruptcy came in 1923. The railroad continued to operate in receivership. Another branch, the four-mile extension from Carrabasset to Bigelow, was given up in 1926 [51].

Already burdened by heavy debts—many imposed by the parent Maine Central—the SR&RL could not survive the Great Depression. Fifty-four miles of track were abandoned in 1933, including the Phillips-Rangley main line of the old Phillips & Rangley [71-75]. The remainder of the system struggled on until 1935 when the line suspended service and the railroad became the property of a local junk dealer, who removed the tracks the following year [94, 95].

The Sandy River system was the largest but by no means the only two-foot railroad in Maine. The Bridgton & Saco River Railroad was launched in 1881 to connect Bridgton Junction on the Maine Central with Bridgton, a town on Long Lake sixteen miles away. The line was completed within two years. Lumber traffic helped the Bridgton & Saco River prosper in the 1890s, and in 1898 it was extended another five miles to Harrison. The line was independently owned and operated until 1912, when the Maine Central acquired control. Business remained substantial until the 1920s, but afterwards its fortunes declined rapidly, and the railroad was forced into bankruptcy in 1927. The following year it was reorganized as the Bridgton & Harrison. In 1931 the five-mile Harrison extension was abandoned [59], but the rest of the railroad hung on until 1941 [160].

The Wiscasset & Quebec was chartered in 1854 as the Kennebec & Wiscasset Railroad. For the next forty years the charter sat unused and the railroad remained unbuilt. In 1892 the charter was revived by the Wiscasset & Quebec Railroad, a little road with ambitious dreams. From the coastal town of Wiscasset it planned to drive northwest toward the Canadian border. Construction started in 1894. A year later the line was opened to Albion, forty-four miles away. By 1897 the tracks had been pushed another eleven miles to Burnham, but the Maine Central refused permission to cross its tracks, and the extension never opened [13]. A fifteen-mile branch was constructed in 1898-99 to Winslow, across the Sebasticook River from Waterville. The Wiscasset & Quebec began to build a bridge into Waterville, but burdened by construction debts and stymied by opposition from the Maine Central, the railroad collapsed into bankruptcy. In 1901 it was reorganized as the Wiscasset, Waterville & Farmington (though it only reached the first-named city). The Winslow branch, never completed to Waterville, was abandoned in two parts in 1912 and 1916 [21, 23]. The remaining portion of the railroad managed to continue operations until the Depression. A derailment on June 15, 1933, brought an end to service, and the line was dismantled in 1934 [82].

The shortest of the two-footers, the five-mile Kennebec Central, received its charter in 1889 and commenced operating the following year. Unconnected to any other railroad, the Kennebec Central ran from Randolph (across the Kennebec River from Gardiner) to Togus, the site of the National Soldiers' Home. During its first decade, it enjoyed prosperity fueled by heavy passenger traffic to and from the Home. Passenger traffic dwindled following the construction of a competing trolley line after the turn of the century, but a lucrative government contract to supply the home with coal kept the railroad in business. When the contract was given to trucks in the spring of 1929, the railroad lost two-thirds of its revenue. Operations were suspended that summer, and the tracks were removed four years later [56]. The Kennebec Central was unusual among abandoned railroads in that it had never operated in the red. Its owners had decided to quit while they were still ahead.

The longest lived of the two-footers was only a bit larger than the Kennebec Central. The Monson Railroad was chartered in the fall of 1882 and completed a year later. It ran six miles from Monson Junction on the Bangor & Piscataquis Railroad (later part of the Bangor & Aroostook) to Monson. Slate from quarries near Monson was always its primary commodity. In its early years the road was only marginally successful, and in 1903 it was purchased by the Monson Slate Company, its primary shipper. The little railroad continued to haul passengers with its antiquated rolling stock until 1938. Slate runs became less frequent and finally ceased altogether in 1942. Formal abandonment came two years later [187]. The two-foot era had ended.

The two-footers would exist only in photographs and memories had it not been for Ellis D. Atwood. In the 1940s Atwood bought the rolling stock of defunct two-foot gauge railroads, including the Monson, the Bridgton & Harrison, and the Sandy River, from scrap dealers and moved it to his 1800-acre cranberry plantation at South Carver, Massachusetts. The railroad that Atwood constructed there, the five-mile Edaville (from his initials) Railroad, rapidly evolved from working road to a prime tourist attraction. Unfortunately, the Edaville Railroad and museum closed in the early 1990s. In 1994 a group of Portland businessmen led by Phineas Sprague, Jr., acquired most of the Edaville rolling stock and returned it to Maine. Visitors to Portland can view and ride the two-foot gauge trains at the Maine Narrow Gauge Railroad & Museum. According to recent reports, an attempt is being made to restore the Edaville Railroad to operation.

3

Finding Lost Railroads

WHEREVER YOU TRAVEL in New England, abandoned railroads are close at hand. But finding lost rail lines is not always easy. Old railroad beds are often so choked with weeds and brush as to be unrecognizable. Many a right of way has been taken over by highways, utility companies, transit lines, or hiking trails. Some no longer exist.

The maps in this book show all railroads in the six New England states, both extant and abandoned, as of the beginning of 1995. More detailed maps may be required to identify some routes. Most useful for this purpose are the 7-1/2 and 15 minute quadrangle topographic maps published by the U.S. Geological Survey. These highly detailed charts, which show all geographical features, including roads, streams, vegetation, contour lines, buildings, and place names, also indicate both active and abandoned railroads. Topographic maps can be purchased from the U.S. Geological Survey, Distribution Branch, Box 25286, Federal Center, Denver, CO 25286 (phone number 800-872-6277). These maps may also be purchased at commercial dealers or consulted at libraries.

Some abandoned rail lines cannot be found on topographic maps. Most often this is because the right of way has been at least partially obliterated or given over to another function. Older topographic maps can often help in these cases. Some libraries retain topographic maps that date back to the 1880s, and these can be used to locate most lines. Comparison with more recent maps will usually reveal what has happened to the old right of way.

Abandoned in 1982, the right of way of the old Worcester, Nashua & Portland division of the B&M in Groton, Mass., is now state-owned, awaiting conversion into a bicycling trail (see line 342).

What once was the roadbed of the Worcester, Nashua & Portland division main line of the B&M in Pepperell, Mass., is now used by hikers, bikers, and snowmobiles (see line 342).

In recent years the recreational potential to hikers, bikers, and horseback riders of abandoned rail lines has attracted increased attention in all parts of the country. After an initial lag, the New England states have built a number of recreational trails and bike paths on former rail right of ways. Even more are in the planning stages. An excellent guide to some of the more popular of these old rail beds is Craig Della Penna's recent *Great Rail-Trails of the*

rail beds is Craig Della Penna's recent *Great Rail-Trails of the Northeast* (Amherst: New England Cartographics, 1995). Congress has passed legislation, upheld by the Supreme Court, which removes some of the legal difficulties in converting old rail lines to trails. A national organization, the Rails-to-Trails Conservancy (Suite 300, 1400 16th Street NW, Washington, DC 20036), promotes the reuse of rail right of ways.

Readers are cautioned that merely because a rail line is abandoned it is not necessarily public property. Indeed, identifying the ownership of lost railroads, particularly those abandoned years ago, is often difficult in the field. In many cases the right of way has reverted to abutting property owners or has been sold to private parties. In these cases, I urge readers to respect the rights of the owners. When in doubt about ownership of a former rail line, consult the local assessor's office.

The ownership of a rail line can be complex. For example, the B&M abandoned its former Milford branch from Shirley through Groton, Pepperell, and Hollis in 1939 and 1942, except for a short segment in front of the Pepperell station, which was used as a wye until the early 1980s [lines 146, 166, 342]. Much of the right of way through Groton has been obliterated and, in some places, built upon. From Groton to the Pepperell station most of the right of way is owned by a power company. The Pepperell station, nicely restored, is privately owned. The former right of way in front of the station was bought by the town of Pepperell in 1985. The B&M railroad—more than half a century after abandonment—still owns the next half mile of right of way. The rest of the line in Pepperell is owned by the state Division of Fisheries & Wildlife. The Beaver Brook Reservation, a publicly-accessible conservation trust, owns some of the right of way in Hollis.

Divided ownership is typical of older rail lines. In recent years many New England states have acquired right of ways intact as the lines become abandoned or even before. In Massachusetts, for example, state law requires a railroad disposing of an unneeded right of way to gave the state the first chance to purchase the land, and next, the municipalities in which it is located, before it can be conveyed to a private party.

The lost railroads of New England await you. Good hunting!

4

Rail Abandonments in New England, 1848-1994

T HE FOLLOWING directory was assembled from many sources. I relied most heavily on the permissions to abandon reported in the published *Reports of Decisions of the Interstate Commerce Commission (ICCR)* (1919-80); the annual listings of rail abandonments that appeared in *Railway Age* from 1917 to 1949; and the weekly listings of abandonments in *Traffic World* from 1950 to 1983, and reports of abandonments in the *Federal Register* (1983-1995). Some of these sources contain errors and omissions (particularly *Railway Age*), and none of them report pre-World War I abandonments.

These four basic sources were supplemented by information gleaned from examination of various atlases and U.S. Geological Survey topographic maps, the annual reports of railroads and state railroad commissions (which themselves contain helpful maps), various editions of the *Official Guide of the Railways* and Poor's *Manual of the Railroads of the United States*, state rail plans, and the reports of various government agencies, such as the U.S. Railway Association. The various books and articles listed in the bibliography were also very useful, particularly for older abandonments.

This list is confined to abandonments by common-carrier steam railroad lines in the six New England states. Excluded are electric and tram lines (except electrified steam railroads operated as integral parts of steam systems), including former steam lines converted to

The New York & New England Railroad once crossed the Housatonic River here at Southbury, Conn., on its route between Waterbury and Poughkeepsie, N.Y. The line was abandoned in 1948 (see line 193).

trolley use without abandonment; cog railways and inclines; segments under one half mile in length; industrial, mining, and logging railroads (for the latter, see C. Francis Belcher, *Logging Railroads of the White Mountains*, Boston: Appalachian Mountain Club, 1980); industrial spurs and yard trackage; minor relocations and realignments, including most urban trackage; and lines never completed (e.g., the Southern New England). In a departure from the first edition, I no longer list those lines that were once abandoned but are now back in service (e.g., the ex-Rutland lines). Missing line numbers in the directory generally are those assigned in the first edition to lines that are now back in service or lines erroneously listed in that edition.

Since many years can pass between the end of train service and the removal of the rails, all dates must be considered approximate. In most cases the year given indicates the date in which the abandonment order became effective. The notes indicate the dates of discontinuation of service and removal of the rails, if known.

Abandonments of former Penn Central lines and many of the B&M lines purchased by the MBTA or the Commonwealth of Massachusetts are particularly difficult to date accurately. Penn Central lines not included in Conrail in 1976 can be abandoned without notifying the federal government and thus announcements of their abandonment do not appear in the *Federal Register* or *Traffic World*. Freight service over most MBTA lines is provided by a rail carrier under contract. If this service ends the MBTA can apply to have the line officially discontinued, at which time the rails can be removed. I consider this to be tantamount to abandonment.

All this has clouded the distinction between "discontinuance" of a line and "abandonment." There are rail lines in which trees are growing through the rails and which grade crossings have long been paved over, but are not legally abandoned, merely "out of service." Few if any of these lines will probably ever see trains again, yet I am reluctant to include them here. Only in cases where the rails are known to have been entirely removed have I considered them abandoned.

Railroad Abbreviations

AV	Aroostook Valley
B&A	Boston & Albany
B&B	Billerica & Bedford
B&C	Barre & Chelsea
B&G	Bennington & Glastenbury
B&H	Bridgton & Harrison
B&L	Boston & Lowell
B&M	Boston & Maine
BAR	Bangor & Aroostook
BOM	Bangor, Oldtown & Milford
BRBL	Boston, Revere Beach & Lynn
BRI	Bristol
BRL	Burlington & Lamoille
BWPS	Boston, Winthrop & Point Shirley
C&C	Claremont & Concord
C&P	Clarendon & Pittsford
CN	Canadian National
CNE	Central New England
CNP	Concord & Portsmouth
CP	Canadian Pacific
CR	Conrail
CV	Central Vermont
D&H	Delaware & Hudson
F&M	Franklin & Megantic
H&W	Hardwick & Woodbury
HB	Harvard Branch
HTW	Hoosac Tunnel & Wilmington
KC	Kennebec Central
KNX	Knox
LAN	Lancaster
LVE	Lamoille Valley Extension
M&B	Montpelier & Barre
MB	Medway Branch
MC	Maine Central
MD&G	Manchester, Dorset & Granville
MON	Monson
MV	Martha's Vineyard
NAN	Nantucket
NB&T	New Bedford & Taunton
NH	New York, New Haven & Hartford
NHC	New Hampshire Central
NHN	New Haven & Northampton
NP	Narragansett Pier
NYNE	New York & New England
OOJ	Old Orchard Junction
P&W	Providence & Worcester
PC	Penn Central
RUT	Rutland
S&E	Sanford & Eastern
SJL	St. Johnsbury & Lake Champlain
SJLC	St. Johnsbury & Lamoille County
SR	Sandy River
SRRL	Sandy River & Rangeey Lakes
ST	Springfield Terminal
SV	Suncook Valley
UF	Union Freight
VT	Vermont
W&Q	Wiscasset & Quebec
WARW	Warwick
WOOD	Woodstock
WEST	West River
WOLF	Wolfboro
WR	White River
WRB	Wood River Branch
WWF	Wiscasset, Waterville & Farmington
YHB	York Harbor & Beach

NOTE: In the following directory "Length: " is the mileage of the abandoned segment.

1

Wilmington, MA   Wilmington Jct., MA
Abandoned: 1848   **Railroad:** B&M   **Length:** 3   **Opened:** 1836
This line was constructed as part of the original Andover & Wilmington RR (which became the B&M in 1842). It provided the connection to the Boston & Lowell RR by which it reached Boston. When the B&M opened its own route into Boston in 1845 it no longer used this connection with the B&L. For three years the B&L operated it until the B&M removed the tracks in 1848. In 1874 the B&L built a branch line that closely paralleled this route, which remains in use today (the "Wildcat Branch").

1A

Ballardvale, MA   North Andover, MA
Abandoned: 1848   **Railroad:** B&M   **Length:** 9.5   **Opened:** 1837
The Andover & Wilmington was chartered in 1833 to construct an eight-mile branch line from the uncompleted Boston & Lowell RR at Wilmington to Andover. The initial segment was completed in 1836, and extended to Bradford in 1837. In 1842 this became part of the original B&M. The establishment of Lawrence in 1846 caused the B&M in 1848 to relocate their main line to the west to pass through (South) Lawrence, and this segment was abandoned. Nearly 150 years later some parts of the right of way in Andover are still visible. In North Andover, Waverly Rd. (formerly Railroad Ave.) follows the old right of way.

2

Harvard Yard (Cambridge), MA   Somerville, MA
Abandoned: 1855   **Railroad:** HB   **Length:** 0.7   **Opened:** 1849
The Fitchburg RR operated this locally-owned short line until 1855 when it was abandoned and the rails removed. No trace of it remains.

3

North Weare, NH   Henniker, NH
Abandoned: 1858   **Railroad:** NHC   **Length:** 7   **Opened:** 1850
The New Hampshire Central RR built this as part of its line from Manchester to Henniker. In 1853 it merged with the Concord & Claremont RR to form the Merrimac & Connecticut Rivers RR. When the merger fell apart in 1858, this line was no longer needed and was abandoned. Rebuilt by the B&M in the 1890s, it was abandoned a second time in 1937 (see line 101).

4

Candia, NH   Suncook, NH
Abandoned: 1862   **Railroad:** CNP   **Length:** 10   **Opened:** 1852
This segment was built as part of the original main line of the Portsmouth & Concord RR. In 1855 the railroad failed and was reorganized as the Concord & Portsmouth. Three years later the line was leased to the Concord RR. In 1861, when the lease expired the Concord demanded that Concord & Portsmouth abandon its line into Concord and in its place construct a branch to Manchester, where the only railroad with which it would connect would be the Concord. When the new line to Manchester opened in 1862 this line was abandoned.

5

North Wrentham (Norfolk), MA   Medway, MA
Abandoned: 1864   **Railroad:** MB   **Length:** 3.6   **Opened:** 1852
Built by local investors to connect Medway with the Norfolk County RR (opened 1849), this short line became obsolete in 1861 when the New York & Boston RR (later the New York & New England) opened its own line through Medway.

6

Bangor, ME   Milford, ME
Abandoned: 1870   **Railroad:** BOM   **Length:** 12   **Opened:** 1855
Maine's first railroad, the Bangor & Piscataquis Canal & RR Co., opened between Bangor and Old Town in 1836. It became the Bangor, Old Town & Milford RR in 1858, but eventually succumbed to competition from the European & North American RR (later MC), which purchased and abandoned it.

7

Simsbury, CT   Tariffville, CT
Abandoned: ca. 1869   **Railroad:** NHN   **Length:** 1   **Opened:** 1850
The New Haven & Northampton RR built this short branch. It was abandoned around 1869, and the right of way was sold to the Connecticut Western RR who incorporated it into their main line between Hartford and the Hudson River. It was abandoned a second time in 1937 (see line 67).

8

Lancaster, MA   Hudson, MA
Abandoned: 1873   **Railroad:** LAN   **Length:** 8
Completed in 1873 by local interests, this short line was intended to be operated jointly by the Fitchburg RR and the Worcester & Nashua RR. The arrangement fell through, and the railroad was never operated for revenue service. It was sold at foreclosure in 1883, and the rails were removed sometime afterwards.

8A

South Berwick (Cummings), ME   South Berwick Jct., ME
Abandoned: 1879   **Railroad:** B&M   **Length:** 2   **Opened:** 1843
This short extension was constructed by the B&M to connect with the Portland, Saco & Portsmouth RR, by which it reached Portland. The B&M leased the latter road in conjunction with the Eastern RR. When the Eastern obtained exclusive control of the Portland, Saco & Portsmouth the B&M built its own line into Portland in 1873, which made this segment obsolete. It was taken out of service shortly thereafter, and the tracks were taken up in 1879.

8B

Weir Village, MA   Old Brewery Wharf, MA
Abandoned: ca. 1873   **Railroad:** NB&T   **Length:** 1   **Opened:** 1847
This freight-only branch became superfluous in 1866 when the Old Colony & Newport RR built its Dighton & Somerset line parallel to this one a thousand feet away. Since the same customers now had access to a through line, this branch lost most of its business and was abandoned around 1873.

9

North Billerica, MA   Bedford, MA
Abandoned: 1878   **Railroad:** B&B   **Length:** 8.3   **Opened:** 1877
New England's first two-foot gauge railroad, the B&B operated only 6 months. The Boston & Lowell built a branch that followed most of this right of way in 1889; most of it was abandoned in 1962 (see line 234).

9A

Dedham, MA   Islington, MA
Abandoned: 1883   **Railroad:** NYNE   **Length:** 1   **Opened:** 1849
The Norfolk County RR opened a rail line from Dedham to Blackstone in 1849. This became the Boston & New York Central RR in 1853, which in 1855 opened its own route (the Midland RR) to Boston. This section between Islington and Dedham was now a seldom used branch (although between 1858 and 1867 it was used to access Boston when the Midland route was not being operated). No passenger trains appear to have used the route after 1867. The line eventually became part of the New York & New England RR, which built its own line to Dedham in 1881. After the abandonment the New York & New England in 1890 virtually rebuilt this line (although it used a closely parallel right of way); the second line was abandoned in 1932 (see line 70).

9B

Crescent Beach, MA   Ocean Spray, MA
Abandoned: 1885   **Railroad:** BWPS   **Length:** 2.5   **Opened:** 1884
This short-lived line was built to connect the Eastern RR with the beaches at Winthrop. Construction began in 1881 and was finished to Ocean Spray the following year, but not operated. In June 1884 the railroad finally began service. It ran for only two seasons before suffering severe damage from a November gale in 1885. It never operated again.

9C

PS&P Jct., ME   Old Orchard Beach, ME
Abandoned: 1885   **Railroad:** OOJ   **Length:** 2.5   **Opened:** 1881
This short line was built to serve the popular seaside resort of Old Orchard Beach. It operated for only two summers, 1881 and 1882, before competition from an existing line proved too much.

10

Maquam (Swanton), VT   Rouses Point, NY
Abandoned: 1888   **Railroad:** LVE   **Length:** 12   **Opened:** 1884
In 1845 the Northern RR of NY constructed its line from Ogdensburg, NY, to Rouses Point, on Lake Champlain. The Northern was reorganized as the Ogdensburg RR in 1858, and then the Ogdensburg & Lake Champlain in 1865. The Ogdensburg & Lake Champlain obtained a charter in the 1870s to construct the Lamoille Valley Extension RR eastward across Lake Champlain from Rouses Point to Maquam, VT, where it would connect with what would become the St. Johnsbury & Lake Champlain. This would parallel the existing Central Vermont line between Rouses Point and Swanton, thus cutting the CV out of what was anticipated to be significant east-west traffic across the lake. Opposition from the CV and a lack of funds apparently prevented construction, but once William H. Vanderbuilt took control of the Ogdensburg & Lake Champlain the line was finally built.

The LVE opened January 1884, and was leased to the Ogdensburg & Lake Champlain, but service on this line was suspended a few months later, apparently because of a court injunction obtained by CV. The CV then acquired the LVE and the line was never again operated.

10A

Point Shirley, MA   Cottage Hill, MA
Abandoned: 1888   **Railroad:** BRBL   **Length:** 0.8   **Opened:** 1884
The Boston, Winthrop & Point Shirley built a standard-gauge line to Point Shirley in Winthrop in 1882 but did not operate it. In late 1883 this became the Boston, Winthrop & Shore RR, which also operated a narrow gauge line. Both the standard and the narrow gauge lines shared a right of way between Ocean Spray and Point Shirley. Both lines finally began operating to Point Shirley in 1884. Two years later the Boston, Winthrop & Shore was leased to the Boston, Revere Beach & Lynn, which abandoned both lines to Point Shirley in 1888.

10B

Charles River, MA   Ridge Hill, MA
Abandoned: 1889   **Railroad:** NYNE   **Length:** 2   **Opened:** 1879
Built to serve a resort hotel at Ridge Hill farms, this obscure branch was operated summers-only until about 1885, and abandoned in 1889.

11

Burlington, VT   Essex Jct., VT
Abandoned: ca. 1890   **Railroad:** BRL   **Length:** 10   **Opened:** 1877
The Burlington & Lamoille RR had constructed this line as part of a 26-mile route from Burlington to Cambridge Jct. When the railroad was leased to the CV in 1889, this segment closely paralleled an existing CV line. Seeing no need for two lines between Burlington and Essex Jct., the CV abandoned this track.

11A

Bennington, VT   Glastenbury, VT
Abandoned: 1890   **Railroad:** B&G   **Length:** 9   **Opened:** 1873
This short line was operated for less than twenty years. It was built to connect Glastenbury's industry with the railroad at Bennington. Part of its right of way was later incorporated into a trolley line.

11B

Revere, MA   Saugus River Jct., MA
Abandoned: 1891   **Railroad:** B&M   **Length:** 4.5   **Opened:** 1881
The Eastern RR constructed its Chelsea Beach Branch in 1881 shortly before it was taken over by the B&M. This operated summers-only for ten years until its abandonment. Some of the track remained in placed unused until the mid 1920s.

11C

Crescent Beach, MA   Point of Pines, MA

Abandoned: 1892   **Railroad:** BRBL   **Length:** 2.5   **Opened:** 1884

The Boston, Winthrop & Point Shirley RR constructed this standard-gauge line in 1881, but was not able to operate it until 1884. The Boston, Revere Beach & Lynn took over operations in 1886 and discontinued operation of the line in 1888.

11D

Nantucket, MA   Surfside, MA   Siasconset, MA

Abandoned: 1895   **Railroad:** NAN   **Length:** 10   **Opened:** 1884

The Nantucket RR, a three-foot narrow gauge line, was opened from Nantucket to Surfside in 1881 and extended to Siasconset in 1884. The line operated summers only until 1894 when the railroad went bankrupt and was shut down. When a new railroad, the Nantucket Central, was organized in 1895, it abandoned this route and constructed a direct inland line between Nantucket and Siasconset, avoiding the pounding waves that had taken their toll on this route.

12

Cottage City, MA   Katama, MA   South Beach, MA

Abandoned: 1896   **Railroad:** MV   **Length:** 8.8   **Opened:** 1876

The Marthas Vinyard RR opened a three-foot gauge railroad between Cottage City and Katama on the island in 1874 and then extended the line via a short spur line to South Beach. It operated summers-only until 1896.

13

Albion, ME   Burnham, ME

Abandoned: 1897   **Railroad:** W&Q   **Length:** 11

The 2-foot gauge W&Q completed this extension of its main line in 1897, but the MC refused it permission to cross its tracks. Unable to acquire the needed rights, the W&Q never operated this line for revenue service. The tracks remained in place unused for several years.

14

Hamilton & Wenham, MA   Asbury Grove, MA

Abandoned: 1901   **Railroad:** B&M   **Length:** 1.1   **Opened:** 1871

The Eastern RR constructed this short branch to serve a Methodist camp meeting. It was operated summers-only until 1901.

15A

West Berlin, MA   Oakdale, MA

Abandoned: 1903   **Railroad:** B&M   **Length:** 7   **Opened:** 1882

The Massachusetts Central RR was chartered in 1869, but did not complete its line from Boston to Northampton until 1887. At first the Boston & Lowell and then the B&M controlled the railroad. This section, which formed part of its main line, was abandoned to construct the Wachusett Reservoir. The B&M built a connection from West Berlin to Clinton where a connection was made with the B&M's Worcester, Nashua & Rochester division. Today, most of this right of way lies under water.

16

Westfield, CT   Cromwell, CT
Abandoned: 1904   **Railroad:** NH   **Length:** 3.5   **Opened:** 1885
The Meriden & Cromwell RR built this line as part of its route from Cromwell to Meriden. In 1888 it became the Meriden, Waterbury & Connecticut River RR and was extended to Waterbury. In 1892 it became one of the final purchases of the ill-fated New York & New England RR. Service was suspended on this segment in 1896 and never resumed.

16A

Curtis St. (East Boston, MA)   Wharf (East Boston, MA)
Abandoned: 1905   **Railroad:** B&M   **Length:** 1   **Opened:** 1838
This was the original main line of the Eastern RR. A ferry connected East Boston with Boston proper. When the Eastern opened its own direct line into Boston in 1854 this became a branch, used mostly for freight (the line was freight-only between 1854 and 1875). In 1905 the B&M (who had operated the line since 1884) decided to abandon the line rather than eliminate grade crossings. A dozen years later the B&M rebuilt part of this branch from Revere to a connection with the Boston & Albany at Curtis St., East Boston, and it remains in use.

17

Mount Abram Jct., ME   Mount Abram, ME
Abandoned: ca. 1905   **Railroad:** F&M   **Length:** 1.7   **Opened:** 1886
This short 2-foot gauge branch line was used mostly to haul lumber.

18

Bethel, CT   Hawleyville, CT
Abandoned: 1911   **Railroad:** NH   **Length:** 6   **Opened:** 1872
Built by the Danbury & Norwalk RR as an extension of the Shepaug RR (Hawleyville-Litchfield), this line was leased to Shepaug, Litchfield & Northern RR (successor to the Shepaug Valley) in 1892. Along with the Shepaug it became part of the New Haven system in 1898. Around 1908 its remaining trains were rerouted via Danbury and the line was taken out of service.

19

Victory, VT   East Haven, VT
Abandoned: 1909   **Railroad:** SJL   **Length:** 6.1   **Opened:** 1882
Built around 1882, this branch was constructed to reach a private lumbering railroad at East Haven.

20

Nantucket, MA   Siasconsett, MA
Abandoned: 1918   **Railroad:** NAN   **Length:** 9.1   **Opened:** 1895
The Nantucket Central built this route to replace its original shore line. This three-foot narrow gauge railroad became the Nantucket RR in 1910. It operated summers only until 1917. When it shut down that September the line closed for good. The tracks were gone by the following summer.

21

Winslow, ME   North Vassalboro, ME
Abandoned: 1912   **Railroad:** WWF   **Length:** 4   **Opened:** 1899
The 2-foot gauge Wiscasset & Quebec RR built this line as part of its Winslow Branch,. The railroad reorganized as the Wiscasset, Waterville & Farmington in 1901. Hampered by its failure to cross the Kennebec River into Waterville, the line was unsuccessful and was abandoned only 13 years after its construction.

21A

Derby Jct., CT   Ansonia, CT
Abandoned: ca. 1912   **Railroad:** NH   **Length:** 3   **Opened:** 1849
This formed port of the original main line of the Naugatuck RR from Devon (near Bridgeport) to Waterbury and Winsted. It ran along the south side of the Naugatuck River. In 1871 the New Haven & Derby RR opened its line from New Haven through Derby Jct. to Ansonia, along the north bank of the Naugatuck. The New Haven RR acquired the Naugatuck in 1887 and the New Haven & Derby in 1892. It had no use for two lines between Derby and Ansonia, and it rerouted all Naugatuck traffic over the New Haven & Derby line. This line appears to have been abandoned around 1912. Flood control projects and other construction have obliterated nearly all traces of it.

21B

Cumberland Jct., ME   Mill Rd. (Gray), ME
Abandoned: ca. 1912   **Railroad:** MC   **Length:** 6   **Opened:** 1871
Originally this line formed part of the MC's line to Danville. This was replaced by a new line approximately a mile and a half to the east from Royal Jct. to Gray (Mill St.) around 1911 and this line was abandoned.

21C

Athol Jct. (East Springfield), MA   Forest Lake Jct. (Bondsville), MA
Abandoned: 1913   **Railroad:** HAMP   **Length:** 14.8
The NH obtained a charter for the Hampden RR in 1910 to build a connection with the B&M east of Springfield, MA. At that time both the NH and the B&M were controlled by J.P. Morgan. Construction began in 1911, and the line was virtually completed by 1913. Unfortunately, by this time the B&M and the NH were no longer under common ownership, and neither was interested in operating the line. The line was never used for revenue service. In 1926 the line was finally sold to a scrap dealer who removed the tracks and structures; an electric company acquired the right of way in 1929. During the 1950s some 5 miles of the Massachusetts Turnpike was built over the old right of way in Ludlow. Much of the rest of the right of way remains visible today.

22

Kingfield, ME   Alder Stream, ME
Abandoned: ca. 1916   **Railroad:** SRRL   **Length:** 2.3   **Opened:** 1905
This was the Alder Stream Branch of the 2-foot gauge Franklin & Megantic RR. It was built only for logging and soon became obsolete.

23

Weeks Mills, ME   North Vassalboro, ME
Abandoned: ca. 1916   **Railroad:** WWF   **Length:** 10.9   **Opened:** 1899
The 2-foot gauge Wiscasset & Quebec RR built this line as part of its Winslow Branch,. The railroad reorganized as the Wiscasset, Waterville & Farmington in 1901. Hampered by its failure to cross the Kennebec River into Waterville, the line was unsuccessful and carried little traffic.

24

Saybrook Point, CT   Fenwick, CT
Abandoned: 1917   **Railroad:** NH   **Length:** 1   **Opened:** 1872
The Connecticut Valley RR built this extension of its Hartford-Old Saybrook line to service the swank summer colony of Fenwick. The New Haven RR took over in 1887 and operated it until 1916. On the abandonment of service, Fenwick station was loaded on a flat car and hauled away via the rail line! In 1917 the line (formerly a trestle) was filled in and rebuilt as an automobile road that continues in use.

24A

Swanton, VT   Maquam, VT
Abandoned: ca. 1917   **Railroad:** SJLC   **Length:** 2.3   **Opened:** 1880
This short branch was constructed to connect the Lake Champlain passenger steamers at Maquam with the SJLC at Swanton.

25

North Concord, VT   Victory, VT
Abandoned: ca. 1918   **Railroad:** MC   **Length:** 5.4   **Opened:** 1882
This line, built ca. 1882, was part of a branch line to East Haven. Its primary purpose was to connect with a private lumber railroad at East Haven, and with little local traffic it was unneeded by 1918.

26A

Manchester, VT   Dorset, VT
Abandoned: 1918   **Railroad:** MDG   **Length:** 6   **Opened:** 1903
Owned by the Vermont Marble Co., this short-lived line existed mainly to haul rock. It provided limited passenger service.

26B

Woburn, MA   Horn Pond, MA
Abandoned: 1919   **Railroad:** B&M   **Length:** 0.5   **Opened:** 1854
Built by the Boston Ice Co. as the Horn Pond Branch RR, this line was operated by the Boston & Lowell as a freight-only branch during the ice-cutting season.

27

Greens Farm, ME   Langtown, ME
Abandoned: 1919   **Railroad:** SRRL   **Length:** 4   **Opened:** 1903
The two-foot gauge Philips & Rangley RR built this as part of the Eustis RR, a lumber-hauling subsidiary. It became part of the Sandy River & Rangley Lakes RR in 1908. Abandoned in 1919, the tracks were not removed until the mid-1930s.

28

Bethlehem Jct., NH [1900 ft S]   Profile House, NH
Abandoned: 1921   **Railroad:** B&M   **Length:** 9.1   **Opened:** 1879
The Profile & Franconia Notch RR built this 3-1/2 foot narrow gauge line from the Boston, Concord & Montreal line at Bethlehem Jct. to Profile Notch, the site of several White Mountain resorts. It was operated June-September-only independently for several years, before coming under the control of the B&M. It was converted to standard gauge in 1892. Since passengers provided nearly all of its traffic, it was especially vulnerable to automobile competition.

29

Cherry Mountain, NH   Jefferson, NH
Abandoned: 1921   **Railroad:** B&M   **Length:** 3.5   **Opened:** 1892
Built as a summer-only branch to serve the resort town of Jefferson, this line carried mostly passengers. It was vulnerable to automobile competition.

30

Feeding Hills, MA   Agawam Jct., MA
Abandoned: 1921   **Railroad:** CNE   **Length:** 1.9   **Opened:** 1904
Built by the Central New England RR as part of its Springfield Branch, this was one of the last new rail lines of southern New England. It was operated for barely 17 years before abandonment. The track remained in place unused until 1938.

31

Brownsville Jct., ME   Katahdin Iron Works, ME
Abandoned: 1922   **Railroad:** BAR   **Length:** 8.9   **Opened:** 1882
The Bangor & Katahdin Iron Works RY opened the first 6 miles of its line between Milo Jct. and the Iron Works in 1881 and the rest in 1882. The Bangor & Piscataquis RR leased the line in 1887 and the BAR took over 4 years later. The closing of the Iron Works in 1890 eliminated much of its traffic, but the BAR did not get around to abandoning this portion of the line until 1922. After abandonment, the tracks remained in place. From 1929 to 1933 Mrs. Sara Grey used the line to serve a postal route employing an automobile equipped with flanged wheels. The tracks were finally taken up around 1934.

32

East Millinocket, ME   Medway, ME
Abandoned: 1922   **Railroad:** BAR   **Length:** 0.9   **Opened:** 1907
The east end of the BAR's East Millinocket Branch, this line remained intact for several years after abandonment.

33

Saybrook Point, CT   Saybrook Jct., CT
Abandoned: 1922   **Railroad:** NH   **Length:** 1.5   **Opened:** 1872
This was part of the Saybrook-Fenwick extension of the Connecticut Valley RR. It was taken over by the New Haven RR in 1887. The track was removed in 1924.

34

Larrabees Point, VT   Ft. Ticonderoga, NY
Abandoned: 1923   **Railroad:** RUT   **Length:** 1.1   **Opened:** 1871
The Addison RR built its line through Addison County, VT, and west across Lake Champlain to Ft. Ticonderoga. The Rutland RR leased it before completion in hopes of it becoming a major route to the west, but these dreams never were realized. Most of this abandonment consisted of a 300-foot drawbridge and another 1500 feet of trestle. In 1920 the bridge was declared unsafe and the line taken out of service.

35

South Deerfield, MA   Shelburne Jct., MA
Abandoned: 1923   **Railroad:** NH   **Length:** 6.8   **Opened:** 1881
Built by the New Haven & Northampton RR to gain access to the Fitchburg RR's recently-opened Hoosac Tunnel route, this line became part of the New Haven system in 1887. Traffic never was heavy, and the line was taken out of service in 1919. The tracks were taken up in 1925.

36

Old Orchard Beach, ME   Camp Ellis (Saco), ME
Abandoned: 1924   **Railroad:** B&M   **Length:** 3.8   **Opened:** 1880
Built by the Orchard Beach RR, this summers-only line carried mostly passengers. The B&M took over operation in 1883. After abandonment the line was sold to a local firm but soon discontinued for good.

37

East Farms, CT   Quarry Jct (Meriden), CT
Abandoned: 1924   **Railroad:** NH   **Length:** 11.8   **Opened:** 1888
Built as part of the Meriden, Waterbury & Connecticut RR this line became part of the New York & New England in 1892. Not operated between 1896 and 1898 it became a seldom-used line of the New Haven. Service was suspended in 1917 and the route was abandoned seven years later.

38

Pontiac, RI   Clyde (River Point), RI
Abandoned: 1924   **Railroad:** NH   **Length:** 2.2   **Opened:** 1880
Built as a branch by the New York, Providence & Boston RR, this formed part of a through route between Auburn and Hope. The NH acquired it in 1892. Passenger service ended in 1922; the tracks were removed in 1925 and 1926.

39

Bethlehem Jct., NH   Bethlehem, NH
Abandoned: 1925   **Railroad:** B&M   **Length:** 3.3   **Opened:** 1881
Originally built as the Bethlehem & Maplewood Division of the narrow-gauge Profile & Franconia Notch RR, this summers-only operation was acquired by the B&M and converted to standard gauge in 1895. Bethlehem boasted 28 hotels, but competition from automobiles and buses doomed the line. The track was removed in 1926.

40

Danvers Jct., MA   Stevens (North Andover), MA
Abandoned: 1926   **Railroad:** B&M   **Length:** 14.9   **Opened:** 1848
Part of the main line of the Essex RR between Salem and Lowell, this was operated first by the Eastern RR and after 1884 by the B&M. The track was taken up in 1927.

41

East Milford, NH   Grasmere Jct., NH
Abandoned: 1926   **Railroad:** B&M   **Length:** 18.5   **Opened:** 1900
Built by the B&M as its Manchester and Milford Branch, this line was constructed mostly to prevent the Fitchburg RR from opening its own line. The same year the line opened, the B&M acquired the Fitchburg, eliminating the need for the line. Despite having no real reason to exist and almost no traffic the line held on for 25 years before the B&M threw in the towel. The track remained until 1930.

42

Nashua, NH [1.9 miles S of Union Sta.]   North Acton, MA
Abandoned: 1925   **Railroad:** B&M   **Length:** 18.1   **Opened:** 1873
The Nashua, Acton & Boston RR built this line to compete with the Boston & Lowell for Nashua to Boston traffic. It became part of New Hampshire's Concord RR system and in 1889 the Concord & Montreal, before passing to the B&M in 1895. Unnecessary as a through route, it served a lightly populated rural region. Passenger service ended in 1924, prior to abandonment. The rails were taken up in 1926.

43

Tewksbury Jct., MA   Pikes Siding (Lawrence), MA
Abandoned: 1926   **Railroad:** B&M   **Length:** 6   **Opened:** 1848
The Lowell & Lawrence RR built this line to connect the two premier industrial cities of the Merrimac Valley. It passed to the Boston & Lowell in 1858 and the B&M in 1887. The B&M had its own route between the two cities, but it continued to operate the Lowell & Lawrence. Passenger service ceased in 1924; the tracks were removed in 1928. Abandonment was authorized between Tewksbury Jct. and Pikes Siding only, but the B&M appears to have also quietly abandoned another mile between Tewksbury Jct. and Tewksbury Centre around this same time.

44

Wakefield Jct., MA   South Peabody, MA
Abandoned: 1926   **Railroad:** B&M   **Length:** 6   **Opened:** 1850
Promoters launched the South Reading Branch RR to open another Boston to Salem route that would compete with the Eastern RR. The Eastern acquired the line in self-defense in 1851. It passed to the B&M in 1884. With rural Essex County crisscrossed by other B&M lines, this one made little sense. In 1926 the I.C.C. authorized the abandonment of the entire branch, from Peabody to Wakefield Jct. The initial half mile between Wakefield Jct. and Wakefield Centre remained in use (apparently as yard track) until about 1935. In the 1950s a short portion of the long-abandoned right of way near Montrose was used for Route 128. In the 1960s tracks were re-laid between Peabody and South Peabody to service an industrial park.

45

Wilmington Jct., MA   Tewksbury Jct., MA
Abandoned: 1925   **Railroad:** B&M   **Length:** 3.2   **Opened:** 1850
The Salem & Lowell RR built this as part of its main line, but it was operated by the Lowell & Lawrence RR. It became part of the Boston & Lowell system in 1858 and passed to the B&M in 1887. Another of Essex County's numerous B&M lines, it lost passenger service in 1924 and was abandoned at the end of 1925.

46

Cape Jct. (Sandy Point), ME   Cape Jellison, ME
Abandoned: 1925   **Railroad:** BAR   **Length:** 1.4   **Opened:** 1905
This freight-only branch was built to enable the BAR to reach the wharves at Cape Jellison. These facilities burned in November 1924, and the BAR used its insurance proceeds to extend its lines to new docks at Searsport, a short distance to the west.

47

in Coos Co., NH
Abandoned: 1925   **Railroad:** MC   **Length:** 0.7   **Opened:** 1890
This was a segment of a MC line, constructed by the Hereford RY, from the international boundary at Beecher Falls, VT, to Lime Ridge, Quebec. Most of the line was in Canada, but at one point the tracks crossed back into the U.S. for 0.7 miles and then reentered Canada. No stations were located on the U.S. segment of the line when it was abandoned.

48

Kennebunk, ME   Kennebunkport, ME
Abandoned: 1926   **Railroad:** B&M   **Length:** 4.6   **Opened:** 1883
The B&M leased the Kennebunk & Kennebunkport RR when it completed this short line. Like other beach railroads, most of its traffic consisted of summer passengers to the seashore (although it operated year round). As such, it was particularly vulnerable to automobile and bus competition, and when the B&M applied to abandon, none of its summer residents or the owners of its 22 resort hotels objected.

49

Harrison Square (Dorchester), MA   Milton (Shawmut Jct.), MA
Abandoned: 1926   **Railroad:** NH   **Length:** 2   **Opened:** 1872
In 1872 the Old Colony built the Shawmut Branch, from Harrison Square on its main line to Milton on the Mattapan Branch. In 1924 the Boston Elevated Railway purchased the Shawmut Branch and the outer portion of Mattapan Branch. The ICC granted the NH permission to abandon. Service continued, however, on the Shawmut Branch until September 1926 and to Mattapan (via the Mattapan Branch) until the Boston Elevated opened its Ashmont to Mattapan trolley line in 1929.

51

Carrabasset, ME   Bigelow, ME
Abandoned: 1926   **Railroad:** SRRL   **Length:** 4   **Opened:** 1900
The two-foot gauge Franklin & Megantic RR built this line as an extension. In 1908 it became part of the Sandy River & Rangley Lakes RR.

52

Concord, MA   Reformatory (Prison Station), MA
Abandoned: 1927   **Railroad:** B&M   **Length:** 2.6   **Opened:** 1879
The Boston & Lowell constructed this extension of its Boston-Lexington-Bedford-Concord line under charter as the Middlesex Central RR. Passenger service ended in 1926.

53

Essex, MA   Conomo, MA
Abandoned: 1927   **Railroad:** B&M   **Length:** 0.5   **Opened:** 1887
This extension of the Essex Branch (Hamilton & Wenham-Essex, built 1872) served a few shipyards. In 1925 the B&M sought permission to abandon the entire Essex Branch, but was allowed only to give up the outermost section.

54

Kittery (Navy Yard), ME   York Beach, ME
Abandoned: 1927   **Railroad:** YHB   **Length:** 10   **Opened:** 1887
The York Harbor & Beach RR opened this beach line in 1887. Between 1904 and 1913 it operated summers only. It always operated independently, although all of its equipment was provided by the B&M. Passenger service ceased in 1925. When abandonment of the entire railroad came two years later, the initial mile was turned over to the B&M and retained to provide continued access to the navy yard. The remaining track was not removed until 1940.

54A

White River Jct., VT   Billings Park, VT
Abandoned: 1928   **Railroad:** CV   **Length:** 0.6   **Opened:** 1890
The Central Vermont built this branch as the Fair Grounds Railroad. It was operated only in summers to serve the Vermont Fair. The fair was held each summer between 1890 and 1900, and then resumed in 1907 and lasted until 1928.

56

Randolph, ME   National Soldiers Home (Togus), ME
Abandoned: 1929   **Railroad:** KC   **Length:** 5   **Opened:** 1890
The two-foot gauge Kennebec Central RR opened its line in 1890. Most of its traffic consisted of hauling coal and visitors to the National Soldiers Home in Togus. The line was doomed when the government shifted its coal contract to trucks in 1929. The track was removed in 1933. Today 2.4 miles of the right of way are part of the Old Narrow Gauge Volunteers Nature Trail.

56A

Central Ave. (Milton), MA   Mattapan, MA
Abandoned: 1929   **Railroad:** NH   **Length:** 1.1   **Opened:** 1847
The Dorchester & Milton Branch RR constructed a line from Neponset to Mattapan in 1847, whereupon the Old Colony RR leased it and operated it as its Mattapan Branch. In 1872 the Old Colony built another line, the Shawmut Branch, from Harrison Square on its main line to Milton on the Mattapan Branch. In 1924 the Boston Elevated Railway purchased the Shawmut Branch and the outer portion of Mattapan Branch. The ICC granted the NH permission to abandon. Service continued, however, on the Shawmut

Branch until September 1926 and to Mattapan (via the Mattapan Branch) until the Boston Elevated opened its Ashmont to Mattapan trolley line in 1929.

57

Bristol, VT   New Haven Jct., VT
Abandoned: 1930   **Railroad:** BRI   **Length:** 6   **Opened:** 1892
The Bristol RR connected with Rutland. Primarily a freight hauler, it provided only mixed-train passenger service in its final years.

58

Chester & Becket Jct., MA   Quarries (Becket), MA
Abandoned: 1931   **Railroad:** B&A   **Length:** 5.3   **Opened:** 1897
This freight-only branch of the B&A was built to serve granite quarries. In its final years it was not operated winters, since it was considered not worth the effort to clear snow from the tracks. It was last operated in 1930.

59

Harrison, ME   Bridgton, ME
Abandoned: 1931   **Railroad:** B&H   **Length:** 3.9   **Opened:** 1898
The two-foot gauge Bridgton & Saco River RR (opened in 1883) built this line as part of its extension. It was reorganized as the Bridgton &Harrison in 1928; by 1930 it was out of service.

62

Whitefield Jct., NH   Lancaster, NH
Abandoned: 1941   **Railroad:** B&M   **Length:** 10.5   **Opened:** 1870
This line was built by the Boston, Concord & Montreal RR as an extension of its line between Littleton and Lancaster. It was taken out of service in 1932.

63

High St. Jct., CT   West Simsbury, CT
Abandoned: 1937   **Railroad:** NH   **Length:** 6.8   **Opened:** 1871
Built by the Connecticut Western RR as part of its main line from Hartford to the Hudson River, this eventually became the Central New England RR in 1898. It became part of the New Haven in 1927, at which time passenger service was discontinued. In 1932 freight service ended on most of this segment as well. Today part of the old right of way carries the Stratton Brook Trail.

64

High St. Jct., CT   East Winsted, CT
Abandoned: 1938   **Railroad:** NH   **Length:** 11.3   **Opened:** 1871
Built by the Connecticut Western RR as part of its main line from Hartford to the Hudson, this became the Central New England RR in 1898. In 1927 it was taken over by the New Haven, who discontinued passenger service. Five years later freight service ended as well.

65

West Winsted, CT   East Canaan, CT
Abandoned: 1938   **Railroad:** NH   **Length:** 15.1   **Opened:** 1871
Built by the Connecticut Western RR as part of its main line between Hartford and the Connecticut River, this became part of the Central New England RR in 1898. The New Haven took over in 1927 and abolished passenger service. Five years later freight service ended as well.

67

Tariffville, CT   Simsbury, CT
Abandoned: 1937   **Railroad:** NH   **Length:** 3.3   **Opened:** 1871
Built by Connecticut Western RR as part of its main line from Hartford to the Hudson, this became part of the Central New England RR in 1898. In 1927 the New Haven assumed operation but discontinued passenger service. The line was taken out of service in 1932.

68

Warren, ME   Union, ME
Abandoned: 1932   **Railroad:** KNX   **Length:** 8.5   **Opened:** 1893
Built as the Georges Valley RR this marginal short line was taken over in 1918 by its biggest shipper, the Knox Lime Co. It was renamed the Knox RR the following year. Its primary traffic source was the lime kilns at Union. It was abandoned as a common carrier in 1932, but it continued to operate sporadically for a few more years as an industrial railroad.

69

Brayton, MA   Fall River, MA
Abandoned: 1932   **Railroad:** NH   **Length:** 1.5   **Opened:** 1875
This constituted the old Slades Ferry Bridge and approaching track. The Old Colony RR extended its line from Providence to Warren and Brayton into Fall River by way of a double-decker bridge over the Taunton River (with the railroad on top and a roadway below). The line was electrified in 1900 and the steam trains between Providence and Fall River were replaced by trolleys. The bridge suffered damage in January 1932 and was taken out service; trolley service ended at the same time. The bridge was turned over to the state and converted to exclusively highway use.

70

Dedham, MA   Islington (Westwood), MA
Abandoned: 1932   **Railroad:** NH   **Length:** 1.4   **Opened:** 1890
The New York & New England RR opened a branch from Dedham Jct. to Dedham in 1881, closely paralleling an unused older branch (see line 9A). This enabled the railroad to offer Boston-Dedham service in competition with the Boston & Providence. The NY&NE discontinued service in 1884, but was forced by the state to restore it in 1888. In 1890 the NY&NE built a short connection from the branch to Islington (which formed the west leg of a wye) to enable the Old Colony RR to operate a second Boston to Providence route via Dedham and the Walpole & Wrentham line. The merger of both the Old Colony and the NY&NE into the New Haven system in the 1890s left little use for this branch. Service via the east leg of the wye ended in September 1899 and on the

rest of the branch in 1904. When the long-neglected line was finally abandoned in 1932, part of its right of way was used for US 1.

71

Bracket Jct., ME   No. 6, ME

Abandoned: 1932   **Railroad:** SRRL   **Length:** 4   **Opened:** 1902

The Madrid RR, a two-foot gauge line, built this line, but it was operated by the Philips & Rangeley RR to haul lumber. It became part of the Sandy River & Rangeley Lakes in 1908. It apparently provided scheduled passenger service. The tracks were taken up in 1934.

72

Eustis Jct., ME   Langtown, ME

Abandoned: 1932   **Railroad:** SRRL   **Length:** 6   **Opened:** 1902

This line formed part of the Eustis RR, a freight-only extension of the Phillips & Rangeley RR. Lumber provided most of the traffic. It became part of the Sandy River & Rangeley Lakes RR in 1908. The tracks were removed in 1934.

73

Madrid Jct., ME   Sandy River, ME

Abandoned: 1932   **Railroad:** SRRL   **Length:** 11   **Opened:** 1903

The two-foot gauge Madrid RR, a subsidiary of the Phillips & Rangeley RR, opened the first section of this line between Madrid Jct. and Bracket Jct. in 1902; the rest of the line was built the following year. It was operated only for freight, mostly lumber. It became part of the Sandy River & Rangeley Lakes RR in 1908. The tracks were removed in 1934.

74

Perham Jct., ME   Barnjum, ME

Abandoned: 1932   **Railroad:** SRRL   **Length:** 4   **Opened:** 1912

The Barnjum Branch of the two-foot gauge Sandy River & Rangeley Lakes RR was one of the last of Maine's narrow-gauge lines to be built. The tracks were taken up in 1934.

75

Phillips, ME   Rangley, ME

Abandoned: 1932   **Railroad:** SRRL   **Length:** 29   **Opened:** 1891

This was the main line of the two-foot gauge Philips and Rangeley RR. Its primary traffic was the peculiarly Maine mixture of timber and tourists bound for the resort village of Rangeley. It became part of the Sandy River & Rangeley Lakes RR in 1908. Passenger service was provided until 1931. The tracks came up in 1934.

76

Woodstock, VT   White River Jct., VT

Abandoned: 1933   **Railroad:** WOOD   **Length:** 13.6   **Opened:** 1875

This independently-operated short line was built to access a stand of timber as well as haul farm produce. Both freight and passenger service were provided until the end. The state took part of the right of way for a highway, including the railroad bridge that spanned Quechee Gorge. Today the bridge (built in 1911) still carries US 4.

77

Old Town, ME   South La Grange, ME (2920 ft SE)
Abandoned: 1933   **Railroad:** BAR   **Length:** 14   **Opened:** 1869
Built by the broad-gauge Bangor & Piscataquis RR as part of its main line to Greenville, it was leased by the BAR in 1892. By the time of abandonment its primary traffic, pulpwood, had shifted to trucks, and the line had virtually no customers left.

78

Austin Jct., ME   Kineo, ME
Abandoned: 1936   **Railroad:** MC   **Length:** 51.3   **Opened:** 1907
The Somerset RY built this extension of its Oakland-Bingham line between 1904 and 1907. In 1911 it was taken over by the Maine Central. It served a sparsely populated region that generated a modest traffic, mostly lumber. It was taken out of service in July 1933 and abandoned three years later.

80

Woodland Jct., ME   Princeton, ME
Abandoned: 1935   **Railroad:** MC   **Length:** 10.5   **Opened:** 1856
This line formed part of the Lewy's Island RR , which constructed a railroad between Baring and Princeton. At Baring the line crossed the St. Croix River into New Brunswick and followed the river to Woodland, where it crossed back into Maine and then to Princeton. Lumber provided most of its traffic. In 1870 it became part of the St. Croix & Penobscot RR, and later, in 1898, passed to the Washington County RR and finally, in 1904, the MC. The line was taken out of service in 1933 and abandoned two years later.

81

Rochester, VT   Bethel, VT
Abandoned: 1933   **Railroad:** WR   **Length:** 19.3   **Opened:** 1900
Construction of this short line railroad was begun in the late 1890s by the White River Valley Electric RR, then completed by the White River Valley RR (electric power was never actually used). In 1902 it became the White River RR. It closed down briefly in 1906-07 and later in 1927-28 due to flood damage. Never a prosperous line it, did not survive the depression.

82

Wiscasset, ME   Albion, ME
Abandoned: 1933   **Railroad:** WWF   **Length:** 44   **Opened:** 1895
This two-foot gauge line was built as the Wiscasset & Quebec RR . In 1899 the tracks were extended another 11 miles from Albion to Burhnam but never operated. The railroad was reorganized as the Wiscasset, Waterville & Farmington RR in 1901.

83

Belmont, NH   Belmont Jct., NH
Abandoned: 1934   **Railroad:** B&M   **Length:** 4.2   **Opened:** 1889
The Belmont Branch was built as the Tilton & Belmont RR and leased on completion to the Concord & Montreal RR. It became part of the B&M in 1895. Passenger service ceased in April 1929, and the line was taken out of service in August 1930 and remaining

customers served by trucks. After abandonment, the first half mile remained in service into the 1980s as an industrial spur.

84

Epping, NH   West Gonic, NH
Abandoned: 1935   **Railroad:** B&M   **Length:** 15.8   **Opened:** 1874
The Nashua & Rochester RR built this line as an extension of the Worcester & Nashua RR. After the B&M acquired it in 1886 it formed part of its Worcester, Nashua & Rochester division, part of a through route between Worcester and Rochester. Service on the line ended in March 1934; the tracks were removed in 1936.

85

Hudson, NH   Fremont, NH
Abandoned: 1935   **Railroad:** B&M   **Length:** 20.6   **Opened:** 1874
The Nashua & Rochester RR built this line as an extension of the Worcester & Nashua RR. After the B&M acquired it in 1886, it formed part of its Worcester, Nashua & Portland division, a through route between Worcester and Portland, ME. Service on the line ended in March 1934. The right of way is now used for the multipurpose Rockingham Recreational Trail.

86

Newington, NH   Dover Point, NH
Abandoned: 1934   **Railroad:** B&M   **Length:** 1.7   **Opened:** 1874
This segment consisted of the 1700-foot Dover Point Bridge across Great Bay and 1.4 miles of approach track. It formed part of a line between Dover and Portsmouth. By the 1930s the railroad shared the bridge with a highway. When Portsmouth-to-Dover passenger service ended in January 1933, the B&M also discontinued through freight traffic over the bridge. After the state built a new highway bridge, the railroad bridge no longer had any use and was therefore abandoned.

87

Granite Jct. (Hardwick), VT   Quarry Sta. (Woodbury), VT
Abandoned: 1934   **Railroad:** H&W   **Length:** 8.8   **Opened:** 1896
The freight-only Hardwick & Woodbury RR was built to transport granite, but was operated as a common carrier railroad. When its quarries closed it had no further reason to exist and was thus abandoned. The tracks were taken up in 1937.

88

Bellingham Jct., MA   Woonsocket Jct., MA
Abandoned: 1934   **Railroad:** NH   **Length:** 4.9   **Opened:** 1863
The New York & Boston RR built this segment as part of its line between Boston (Brookline) and Woonsocket. It eventually passed to the New York & New England RR and in 1898 became part of the New Haven system. Both passenger and freight service ended in 1930, but the line was not abandoned until four years later (tracks removed in 1935).

88A

Alburgh, VT   Canadian border
Abandoned: ca. 1934   **Railroad:** RUT   **Length:** 2.4   **Opened:** 1899
This was built as part of the Rutland's great expansion in 1899, which gave it a route to Canada independent of the CV. A short section in Canada, built as the Rutland & Noylan RR, gave it a connection with the Grand Trunk (Canadian National) at Noylan Jct., PQ. By 1919 it was no longer used for scheduled passenger service, and it had little or no freight traffic. It was apparently abandoned around 1934, and the rails were removed around the beginning of the Second World War.

89

Bondsville, MA   Athol, MA
Abandoned: 1935   **Railroad:** B&A   **Length:** 28.5   **Opened:** 1871
The Athol & Enfield RR constructed this line through the valley of the Swift River. In 1873 it was extended to Springfield. Reorganized as the Springfield, Athol & Northeastern and then the Springfield & Northeastern, it was acquired by Boston & Albany in 1880. The B&A operated it as its Athol Branch until the state decided to construct the giant Quabbin Reservoir in the Swift River valley. The artificial lake flooded 16 miles of this segment and left the initial 12 miles south of Athol dry but cut off from the rest of the B&A system. The B&A therefore abandoned the entire segment. Much of this right of way is today under water.

90

Coolridge Crossing (Hancock), NH   Keene, NH
Abandoned: 1938   **Railroad:** B&M   **Length:** 21.9   **Opened:** 1878
The Manchester & Keene RR was chartered in 1864 to connect Greenfield and Keene, but it did not complete its line until 14 years later. Eventually it came to be operated by the Boston & Lowell RR and after 1887 by the B&M. Plagued by heavy grades and few local customers, the line was a marginal operation. Passenger service ended in 1934 after a landslide near Elmwood severed the line into two disconnected segments. Service was discontinued altogether in 1935 to avoid making expensive bridge repairs, and formal abandonment followed three years later.

91

Lilly Pond, NH   Alton, NH
Abandoned: 1935   **Railroad:** B&M   **Length:** 15.9   **Opened:** 1890
Built by the Lake Shore RR and controlled by the Concord & Montreal RR, this line became part of the B&M in 1895. It once carried substantial numbers of passengers to Lake Winnipesaukee summer resorts and lake steamers, but by the 1930s it saw little freight and few passengers. When abandonment came in 1935, the initial 0.6 miles out of Alton were retained, but this track was taken up the following year. The old right of way is still visible along the shore of Lake Winnipesaukee from Route 11 at Belknap Point and Ames Farm.

92

Parkers, NH   New Boston, NH
Abandoned: 1935   **Railroad:** B&M   **Length:** 5.2   **Opened:** 1893
The New Boston RR built this obscure branch line and leased it to the Concord & Montreal RR. It passed to the B&M in 1895. Bad track closed the line in June 1931, and abandonment followed four years later.

93

Oquossoc, ME   Kennebago, ME
Abandoned: 1936   **Railroad:** MC   **Length:** 10.8   **Opened:** 1912
The MC established the Rangeley Lakes & Megantic RR in 1910 to construct this branch line. Its primary traffic was pulpwood, fisherman and hunters. The line was taken out of regular service in July 1933, although some pulpwood was hauled as late as August 1935. For a few years the Kennebago Bus Co. ran motor buses fitted with flanged wheels on the tracks. Major floods in March 1936 damaged the Rumford Falls & Rangeley Lakes RR (see line 99), which it joined at Oquossoc, leaving it without a connection. Abandonment soon followed.

94

Farmington, ME   Phillips, ME
Abandoned: 1935   **Railroad:** SR   **Length:** 18   **Opened:** 1879
This formed part of the original main line of Maine's first two-foot gauge railroad, the Sandy River RR. It used rolling stock from the abandoned Bedford & Billerica RR in Massachusetts. In 1908 it became part of the Sandy River & Rangeley Lakes RR. After many successful years, it did not survive the decline in lumber traffic and the Great Depression. The track was removed in 1936.

95

Strong, ME   Carrabasset, ME
Abandoned: 1935   **Railroad:** SR   **Length:** 24   **Opened:** 1894
The Franklin & Megantic RR opened this two-foot narrow gauge line between Strong and Kingfield in 1883, and through a subsidiary, the Kingfield & Dead River RR, extended it to Carrabassett a decade later. In 1908 it became part of the Sandy River & Rangeley Lakes RR. The track was taken up in 1936.

96

Franklin Falls Dam, NH   Bristol, NH
Abandoned: 1936   **Railroad:** B&M   **Length:** 12.8   **Opened:** 1848
The Franklin & Bristol RR opened this line in 1848, and the following year it became part of the Northern RR. It eventually became a B&M branch in 1890. Severe floods of the Pemigewasset River in March 1936 took the line out of service and the line was put up for abandonment. The track was removed in 1938.

97

Bleachery (Lowell), MA   Wamesit, MA
Abandoned: 1936   **Railroad:** B&M   **Length:** 1.5   **Opened:** 1848
The Lowell & Lawrence RR built this segment as part of its main line between the two Merrimac Valley industrial cities. The Boston & Lowell took over in 1858. The rival B&M

constructed its own Lowell branch in 1874, which closely paralleled this line. When the B&M took over the Boston & Lowell in 1887, it had no need for two lines between Lowell and Lawrence. Passenger service ended on this line in 1895 and by 1900 freight service was gone as well. Legal abandonment, however, was delayed for another 36 years.

98

Elkhurst, VT   Canadian border
Abandoned: 1936   **Railroad:** CP   **Length:** 1   **Opened:** 1910
The CP sponsored the construction of the Orford Mountain RR from eastern Quebec across the international boundary to a connection with the CP's Vermont mainline at Elkhurst, near North Troy, VT. The U.S. portion of the line, only about a mile long, was built by the Midland RY Co. of Vermont, but the line was operated as a single CP branch.

98A

Rockport, ME   Crockets Point (Rockport), ME
Abandoned: 1937   **Railroad:** LR   **Length:** 1.5   **Opened:** 1888
Built to haul lime, the LR was basically an industrial railroad, although it was organized as a common carrier. This section was last used in 1934.

99

Rumford, ME   Oquossoc, ME
Abandoned: 1936   **Railroad:** MC   **Length:** 36   **Opened:** 1905
The Rumford Falls & Rangeley Lakes RR opened a line between Rumford and Bemis in 1898. The line was extended to Oquossoc in 1905, and two years later the entire railroad was leased to the Maine Central. Nearly all traffic on the line was from logging, although a daily passenger train operated through 1935. In that year the line changed to seasonal operation, and was shut down for the year at the end of November. In March 1936 heavy floods partially destroyed a bridge over the Androscoggin River, making it impossible to operate the line. The MC convinced the ICC that the bridge was not worth repairing, and the line was abandoned. The track was removed in 1937.

100

Brattleboro, VT   South Londonderry, VT
Abandoned: 1936   **Railroad:** WEST   **Length:** 36   **Opened:** 1880
The narrow-gauge Brattleboro & Whitehall RR opened its twisting main line in 1880. Steep grades and numerous wooden bridges marked its route. The Central Vermont RR operated the line as its Brattleboro and Whitehall division. In 1905 the CV converted the line to standard gauge, renamed it the West River RR, and continued to operate it until 1927 when floods shut it down. Local businessmen, with the help of the state of Vermont, reopened the railroad as an independent short line in February 1931. Unfortunately, the Great Depression was not conducive to new business ventures and the line was once more shut down in October 1934, this time for good. The initial 7 miles from Brattleboro to West Dummerston, however, were reclassified as industrial track and continued to be operated for a while longer.

101

Goffstown, NH   Henniker Jct., NH
Abandoned: 1937   **Railroad:** B&M   **Length:** 16.4   **Opened:** 1893
This segment formed part of the Manchester-Henniker-North Weare Branch of the B&M. It was built as the New Hampshire Central RR and in 1853 became part of the Merrimac & Connecticut River RR and later part of the Concord & Montreal RR. The B&M acquired the line in 1895. The section between North Weare and Henniker Jct. was abandoned in 1858 (see line 3) and rebuilt in 1891 (although not put in service until 1893). Most of its local traffic came from farms, which by the 1930s were increasingly relying on trucks. The line was badly damaged by the great floods of March 1936 and was never again operated.

102

South Ashburnham, MA   Ashburnham, MA
Abandoned: 1937   **Railroad:** B&M   **Length:** 2.6   **Opened:** 1874
The Ashburnham RR built this line to connect Ashburnham Center with the main line of the Fitchburg RR at South Ashburnham. It was operated without great success as an independent short line until 1885 when the Fitchburg leased the line. It became a B&M branch in 1900. Passenger service ended in 1924. The severe floods of March 1936 shut down the line, and it never reopened. The tracks were taken up in 1938.

103

East Barre, VT   Websterville, VT
Abandoned: 1937   **Railroad:** B&C   **Length:** 1.4   **Opened:** 1894
The East Barre & Chelsea RR constructed this short line to form a connection with the Barre RR. It was leased to the latter line in 1895, and in 1913 it became part of the East Barre branch. It was taken out of service in 1936.

104

Bethel, VT   Ellis Quarry (East Bethel), VT
Abandoned: 1937   **Railroad:** CV   **Length:** 5.4   **Opened:** 1905
The Bethel Granite RY was built as an industrial railroad to serve a granite quarry. It was operated, however, by the CV, who reported it as a common carrier line. It apparently ran no scheduled passenger trains. The line was last operated in November 1933.

105

Allerton Farms (Waterbury), CT [1.6 mi E]   Southbury, CT
Abandoned: 1937   **Railroad:** NH   **Length:** 11.6   **Opened:** 1881
The NY&NE constructed this line as part of its Danbury extension from Waterbury to Brewster, N.Y., and beyond. Confronted by steep grades, the extension took 15 years to complete. After the NY&NE was absorbed by the NH in 1898, however, this line served little purpose. Most through service was rerouted. Passenger service ended in 1932 and by the time of abandonment only one shipper remained. The right of way now carries the Larkin Bridle Trail.

106

Dighton, MA [2500 ft S]   Somerset Jct., MA [2400 ft N]
Abandoned: 1937   **Railroad:** NH   **Length:** 3.2   **Opened:** 1866
The Old Colony & Newport RR built this segment as part of its Dighton & Somerset main line between Boston and Fall River. The Old Colony system became part of the NH in 1893. Passenger and freight trains used the line daily until 1932 when the NH abandoned a drawbridge across the Taunton River. This brought an end to passenger and through freight service. Local freight continued for a few years more south from Dighton and north from Somerset Jct., but traffic was insufficient to justify continuing service. The track was not removed until 1940.

107

East Thompson, CT   Webster, MA [2080 ft E]
Abandoned: 1937   **Railroad:** NH   **Length:** 5.5   **Opened:** 1867
The Boston, Hartford & Erie RR built this line as part of its Southbridge Branch. It became part of the NY&NE in 1875, and after 1898, the NH. Since the NH connected at Webster, this line was no longer needed as a through line to Southbridge. Passenger service ended in 1930. The line was last used in March 1936 when severe floods cut off all other rail routes to Webster.

108

East Warren, RI   Brayton, MA
Abandoned: 1937   **Railroad:** NH   **Length:** 6.3   **Opened:** 1865
The Fall River, Warren & Providence built this segment as part of its through line between Providence and Fall River. Between 1900 and 1932 the line was electrified and passenger service was provided by trolleys. With the end of electric service, the wires were removed and steam-powered freight continued until abandonment.

109

Elmwood, MA   Stanley, MA
Abandoned: 1937   **Railroad:** NH   **Length:** 1.2   **Opened:** 1847
The Old Colony RR built this short segment as part of its Bridgewater Branch (Whitman-Stanley). The NH assumed operation in 1893. Passenger service ended in 1925, and by 1932 the line was no longer in use. Remaining traffic on the Bridgewater Branch had been rerouted via Elmwood and Westdale. The tracks were removed in 1940.

110

Harwich, MA   Chatham, MA
Abandoned: 1937   **Railroad:** NH   **Length:** 7.7   **Opened:** 1887
The Chatham RR constructed this short line, which was leased on completion by the Old Colony RR. The NH took over in 1893 and continued to operate it for passenger and freight until 1931 when passenger service ceased. Light freight traffic continued until abandonment.

111

Hyannis, MA [2140 ft S]   Hyannis Wharf (Hyannis Dock), MA
Abandoned: 1937   **Railroad:** NH   **Length:** 1.2   **Opened:** 1854
The Cape Cod RR constructed this line as the terminal of its original main line from Middleboro. From here ferries departed for Marthas Vinyard and Nantucket. The ferries were moved to Woods Hole in 1872, but other boats connected with trains until 1931, when operation of the line ended.

112

Melrose, CT   Ellington, CT [1800 ft NW]
Abandoned: 1937   **Railroad:** NH   **Length:** 3.3   **Opened:** 1876
The Connecticut Central RR built this segment as part of its Westway Branch, from Melrose to Westway. The NY&NE took over in 1880, and in 1898 it became a branch of the NH. Trolley wire was strung above the tracks in 1907 and electric passenger service continued until the late 1920s. The wires were removed and freight service behind steam locomotives continued. Local traffic to and from this sparsely populated area dwindled to only a few carloads a year. The great floods of March 1936 washed out a culvert between Melrose and Sadds Mills, and this segment was taken out of service. Abandonment of the entire line followed a year later.

113

Middleboro, MA [3700 ft S]   Myricks, MA
Abandoned: 1937   **Railroad:** NH   **Length:** 5.8   **Opened:** 1846
The Fall River RR built this track as part of its main line from Fall River to South Braintree (where it connected with Old Colony RR to reach Boston). The Old Colony took over the Fall River in 1854 and in turn was absorbed by the NH in 1893. In 1931 all Boston-to-Fall River trains were rerouted and passenger service over this segment ended. Freight service was suspended the following year. The rails remained in place until 1940.

114

Nantasket Jct., MA [2530 ft E]   Pemberton, MA
Abandoned: 1938   **Railroad:** NH   **Length:** 7   **Opened:** 1880
The Nantasket Beach RR built a short line to serve beach goers in 1880 but closed in 1886. Until 1881 it was unconnected to any other railroad. The Old Colony reopened the line in 1888. The NH took over in 1893 and two years later electrified the line. Trolleys hauled thousands to and from the beaches until 1932 when the wires came down. Occasional steam-powered passenger excursions and infrequent freight service continued until abandonment.

115

Pascoag, RI   Douglas Jct., MA
Abandoned: 1937   **Railroad:** NH   **Length:** 6.8   **Opened:** 1893
Built by the NY&NE this constituted an extension of its line from Providence to Pascoag. Passenger service was suspended around 1895 and not restored until 1904. The NH took over operation of the line in 1898. Passenger service between Douglas Jct. and Wallum Lake ended in 1921 and on the rest of the line around 1925. All remaining service on the line ceased in July 1926, but the line was not abandoned until 11 years later.

116

Plymouth, MA [2350 ft W]   North Carver, MA [2300 ft E]
Abandoned: 1937   **Railroad:** NH   **Length:** 7.4   **Opened:** 1892
The Old Colony RR built this line as part of the Plymouth & Middleboro RR. The following year it became a branch of the NH. Passenger service ended in 1927, and the sparsely populated countryside through which it passed generated little freight traffic. The line was taken out of service in 1934; the tracks were removed in 1940.

117

Raynham, MA   Dean St. (Taunton), MA [2600 ft N]
Abandoned: 1937   **Railroad:** NH   **Length:** 2.6   **Opened:** 1866
The Old Colony & Newport RR built this segment as part of its Dighton & Somerset main line between Boston and Fall River. In 1882 the Old Colony opened a new station in Taunton on the New Bedford & Taunton line, and nearly all passenger trains were rerouted from this line to the line from Raynham to Whittenton Jct. The NH continued this practice when it took over the OC in 1893. Passenger service ceased altogether around 1916. The line was finally taken out of service entirely in 1932; the tracks were lifted in 1940.

118

Slatersville, MA   Harrisville, RI
Abandoned: 1937   **Railroad:** NH   **Length:** 6.3   **Opened:** 1891
The NY&NE constructed this line as part of an extension from Woonsocket to Pascoag (actually Harrisville; an existing Providence-Pascoag line was used to reach Pascoag). The segment of the line between Glendale and Harrisville (2.8 miles) was taken out of service in April 1925. Passenger service on the entire line ended about the same time. The rest of the line hung on for another dozen years before abandonment.

119

Sterling Jct., MA   Sterling, MA [1600 ft S]
Abandoned: 1937   **Railroad:** NH   **Length:** 2.1   **Opened:** 1850
This line was constructed by the Fitchburg & Worcester RR as part of its main line. The Fitchburg & Worcester operated as an independent line until 1869 when it became part of the Boston, Clinton & Fitchburg RR. This system subsequently was acquired by the Old Colony RR in 1879 and the NH in 1893. Passenger service ended around 1926, and freight service was suspended in 1934; the tracks were finally removed in 1940.

120

Whitman, MA   East Bridgewater, MA
Abandoned: 1937   **Railroad:** NH   **Length:** 3.3   **Opened:** 1847
Built by the Old Colony RR as part of its Bridgewater Branch (Whitman-Stanley), this line passed to the NH in 1893. Passenger service ceased in 1925; the tracks were removed in 1940.

121

at Wilsons Point, CT
Abandoned: 1938 **Railroad:** NH **Length:** 0.6 **Opened:** 1884
This segment constituted the final 0.6 miles of track to the Wilsons Point dock. The line was constructed by the Danbury & Norwalk RR to reach Wilsons Point, reputed to have one of the finest harbors on Long Island Sound. It formed part of a new Boston-New York passenger line, utilizing the NY&NE, the Danbury & Norwalk, and steamships from Wilsons Point to New York City. Barges transported freight cars to New York, Long Island, even New Jersey. This operation came to an abrupt halt in 1892 when the rival NH purchased the Danbury & Norwalk. By 1894 passenger service on the branch was gone, and the line was relegated to a minor branch line. The line was last used in 1933, but formal abandonment was delayed until five years later.

122

Wing Rd., NH   Base, NH
Abandoned: 1938 **Railroad:** B&M **Length:** 20.1 **Opened:** 1876
The White Mountains RR built this line to carry passengers to the Mt. Washington Cog RY at Base. The initial section between Wing Rd. and Fabyans was opened in 1874, and the line was completed to Base two years later. The Boston & Lowell took over the railroad in 1884, and it became a B&M line in 1887. It was taken out of service in July 1932, but the line was not formally abandoned until 1938.

123

Essex Jct., VT   Cambridge Jct., VT
Abandoned: 1938 **Railroad:** CV **Length:** 25.8 **Opened:** 1877
The Burlington & Lamoille RR built this line to connect the new Lamoille Valley RR with the CV. The CV leased the line in 1889. The sparsely settled Vermont countryside produced little traffic, and by the time of abandonment service consisted only of a daily mixed train. At that time 0.9 mile of track at Cambridge Jct. was transferred to the St. Johnsbury & Lake Champlain RR to operate as a spur.

124

Center Rutland, VT   Rutland, VT
Abandoned: 1938 **Railroad:** C&P **Length:** 0.6 **Opened:** 1890
The Pittsford & Rutland RR built this as part of its 1.8 mile-long line around 1890. From the beginning it was leased by the C&P, which eventually purchased it in 1911.

125

Readsboro, VT   Wilmington, VT
Abandoned: 1938 **Railroad:** HTW **Length:** 13 **Opened:** 1891
The narrow-gauge Hoosac Tunnel & Wilmington built this extension of its main line to serve local factories. Converted to standard gauge in 1913, the line was relocated and extensively rebuilt in the 1920s to allow for the construction of Lake Whitingham. A major flood in November 1927 knocked this line out of service for two years and permanently ended passenger service. Additional flooding in March 1936 took out the Deerfield River trestle south of Wilmington, and the line was never operated again.

126

Crowleys Jct., ME   Leeds Jct., ME
Abandoned: 1938   **Railroad:** MC   **Length:** 11.3   **Opened:** 1861
The Androscoggin RR built this extension to reach the seaboard at Brunswick. The section between Sabattus and Leeds Jct. was taken out of regular service in June 1932 and used to store rolling stock.

127

Waukeag, ME   Mt. Desert Ferry, ME
Abandoned: 1938   **Railroad:** MC   **Length:** 2.4   **Opened:** 1884
The Maine Shore Line RR built this line for the MC, and on completion the line was taken over by the MC. It provided access to the wharves where ferries operated to Bar Harbor on Mount Desert Island. The ferry was discontinued in April 1931, leaving only mixed train service on the branch. This ended two years later and the line sat unused until abandonment.

128

Bridgeport, CT [N end yard limit]   Stepney, CT
Abandoned: 1940   **Railroad:** NH   **Length:** 7.4   **Opened:** 1840
This segment once formed the Bridgeport-Pittsfield main line of the Housatonic RR. The Housatonic operated independently until 1892 when it was absorbed by the NH. Passenger service ceased in 1932 and remaining Bridgeport-Pittsfield trains were re-routed by way of Norwalk and Danbury. The line generated little local traffic, but the NH retained it for occasional wide loads.

129

Griffins, CT   Tariffville, CT
Abandoned: 1938   **Railroad:** NH   **Length:** 2.7   **Opened:** 1871
Built by the Connecticut Western RR as part of its main line between Hartford and the Connecticut River, this became part of the Central New England RR in 1898. The New Haven took over in 1927 and abolished passenger service. Five years later freight service ended as well.

130

at High St. Jct. (Collinsville), CT
Abandoned: 1938   **Railroad:** NH   **Length:** 1.2   **Opened:** 1871
Part of the same route as line 129; see the note for that segment.

131

Hopkinton, MA   Ashland, MA
Abandoned: 1938   **Railroad:** NH   **Length:** 4.6   **Opened:** 1872
Built by the Hopkinton Branch RR, this segment eventually became part of the Milford & Woonsocket RR in 1883. The NY&NE took over in 1887 and by 1898 this was a NH branch. After the end of passenger service in 1920, quarries and grain provided most of the traffic until abandonment. The tracks were removed in 1940.

132

Lakeville, CT   State Line, NY
Abandoned: 1938   **Railroad:** NH   **Length:** 2.8   **Opened:** 1871
Part of the same route as line 129; see the note for that segment.

135

Randolph, MA [1780 ft SW]   Stoughton Jct., MA
Abandoned: 1938   **Railroad:** NH   **Length:** 5.1   **Opened:** 1866
The Old Colony & Northern built this segment as part of its Dighton & Somerset main line between Braintree Highlands and Fall River. The NH took over operation in 1893. Passenger service ended around 1927 and through freights were rerouted. Local traffic was insufficient to sustain the line. The rails were not taken up until 1942.

136

Tariffville, CT   Feeding Hills, MA
Abandoned: 1938   **Railroad:** NH   **Length:** 12.4   **Opened:** 1904
The Springfield Branch of the CNE was built to give the east-west CNE access to the B&A and B&M at Springfield. By the time the branch finally opened (after the NH waged a long battle to block its completion) the NH had taken control of the CNE and the line served little purpose. Passenger trains ceased in 1922 and the line north of Feeding Hills was abandoned, leaving this a long branch to Feeding Hills.

137

West Bridgewater, MA   Eastondale, MA
Abandoned: 1938   **Railroad:** NH   **Length:** 3.5   **Opened:** 1888
The West Bridgewater Branch of the Old Colony RR ran from Easton to Matfield. The NH took over the Old Colony in 1892. This was the first of 4 segments to be abandoned; the last went in 1963. The tracks were removed in 1940.

138

West Hanover, MA   Hanover, MA
Abandoned: 1938   **Railroad:** NH   **Length:** 4.2   **Opened:** 1868
This segment was built as part of the Hanover Branch RR, which operated as an independent short line until 1887 when it was taken over by the Old Colony RR. The NH assumed control 5 years later. The tracks between Rockland and West Hanover (1.75 miles) were retained as an industrial spur. The rest of the track was removed in 1940.

139

West Haven, CT   Orange, CT
Abandoned: 1938   **Railroad:** NH   **Length:** 4.8   **Opened:** 1871
The New Haven & Derby RR constructed this segment as part of its New Haven-Derby-Ansonia line. Passenger trains stopped running in 1925.

140

Westfield, CT   York Hill Quarry (Meriden), CT
Abandoned: 1938   **Railroad:** NH   **Length:** 4.9   **Opened:** 1885
This line once constituted part of the Meriden & Cromwell and later the Meriden, Waterbury & Connecticut River, which operated from Cromwell to Waterbury via

Meriden The line was not operated 1896-98, but the NH restored service. In 1906 the NH electrified the line, and electric cars operated between Meriden and Middletown until 1932. Most of the line sat unused until abandonment once electric service ended.

141

Wickford, RI   Wickford Landing, RI
Abandoned: 1938   **Railroad:** NH   **Length:** 0.6   **Opened:** 1871

The Newport & Wickford RR & Steamboat Co. opened this line as part of its branch to connect the New York, Boston & Providence RR with its steamboats on Narragansett Bay. The railroad continued to operate independently until World War I. Both steamboats and passenger trains ceased in October 1925. This segment was taken out of service the following year, although formal abandonment was more than a decade later.

142

Woonsocket Jct., MA   Woonsocket, RI
Abandoned: 1938   **Railroad:** NH   **Length:** 2   **Opened:** 1863

The New York & Boston RR built this segment as part of its line between Boston (Brookline) and Woonsocket. It eventually passed to the New York & New England RR and in 1898 became part of the New Haven system. Both passenger and freight service ended in 1930, but the line was not abandoned until eight years later.

143

Ludlow, MA   Bondsville, MA
Abandoned: 1939   **Railroad:** B&A   **Length:** 10.8   **Opened:** 1873

The Springfield, Athol & Northeastern RR built this line as part of its through route between Athol and Springfield. At the time of abandonment it had been out of service since 1938 due to flood damage. Some 1.5 miles between Barretts Jct. and Bondsville continued to be operated by the CV into the 1950s to serve textile mills.

144

Elmwood, NH   Coolridge Crossing (Hancock), NH
Abandoned: 1939   **Railroad:** B&M   **Length:** 1.8   **Opened:** 1878

This segment once formed part of the Manchester & Keene RR. Run by various operators for five years, it became a Boston & Lowell line in 1883 and part of the B&M in 1887. Passenger service was discontinued in 1934. The heavy flooding that accompanied the great hurricane of September 1938 damaged the line and it was taken out of service.

145

Oakdale, MA   Wheelwright, MA
Abandoned: 1939   **Railroad:** B&M   **Length:** 24.2   **Opened:** 1887

This was constructed between 1878 and 1887 as part of the Boston- to-Northampton main line of the Massachusetts Central (later Central Massachusetts) RR. It was operated briefly by the Boston & Lowell RR before becoming part of the B&M in 1887. Passenger service ended in 1932. The portion of the line between Oakdale and Rutland was taken out of service in June 1938; the torrential rains that followed in the wake of the great hurricane that September caused flooding that closed the rest of the line.

146

Pepperell, MA   South Milford, NH
Abandoned: 1939   **Railroad:** B&M   **Length:** 13.3   **Opened:** 1895
The Fitchburg RR sponsored the construction of this line as part of a route from Ayer, Mass., to Milford, NH. The Brookline & Pepperell and Brookline Railroads opened a line from Squannacook Jct. (near Ayer) to Brookline, NH., in 1892. Two years later the Brookline & Milford RR completed the line to Milford. Beyond Pepperell the prime traffic source was a commercial ice operation that harvested ice from a pond in Brookline. The B&M took over the line in 1900. Passenger service ceased in 1931. The following years the tracks north of Brookline were taken out of service. When a fire destroyed the Brookline ice house in 1935, there were no regular customers left on the line. After a final shipment in 1937, the line was shut down and abandoned two years later.

147

South Middleton, MA [2000 ft W]   Wilmington Jct., MA
Abandoned: 1939   **Railroad:** B&M   **Length:** 7   **Opened:** 1850
This was part of the Salem & Lowell RR's main line between its namesake cities. It was operated first by the Lowell & Lawrence RR and after 1858 by the Boston & Lowell. It became a branch of the B&M in 1887. Passenger service ended in 1932.

148

South Barre, VT   Williamstown, VT
Abandoned: 1939   **Railroad:** CV   **Length:** 3.9   **Opened:** 1888
The CV built this line as an extension of its Barre branch. Passenger service ended in 1938.

149

at Bristol, RI
Abandoned: 1939   **Railroad:** NH   **Length:** 0.5   **Opened:** 1855
The Providence, Warren & Bristol RR built its original line into Bristol from Providence. This railroad continued to operate the line until 1891 when the Old Colony RR and later the NH took over. The line was electrified between 1900 and 1934. Passenger service with gas electric cars continued until 1937.

151

Greenbush, MA [2100 ft S]   Kingston, MA
Abandoned: 1939   **Railroad:** NH   **Length:** 14.2   **Opened:** 1874
Built by the Duxbury & Cohasset RR, this formed part of a through line between Braintree and Kingston. The section between Greenbush and South Duxbury was completed in 1871; the remainder of the line opened 3 years later. The Old Colony RR took control of the line in 1878, and it passed to the NH in 1893. Objections were heard when the NH filed to abandon the line, but the commuters and small shippers who used the railroad were not deemed sufficient to retain the line.

152

Middleboro, MA   North Carver, MA [2300 ft E]
Abandoned: 1939   **Railroad:** NH   **Length:** 7.6   **Opened:** 1892
The Old Colony RR built this line as part of the Plymouth & Middleboro RR. The following year it became a branch of the NH. Passenger service ended in 1927, and the sparsely populated countryside through which it passed generated little freight traffic.

153

Franklin, NH   Franklin Falls Dam, NH
Abandoned: 1940   **Railroad:** B&M   **Length:** 2.5   **Opened:** 1848
The Franklin & Bristol RR opened this line in 1848, and the following year it became part of the Northern RR. It eventually became a B&M branch in 1890.

154

Adamsdale, MA   Franklin Jct., MA
Abandoned: 1941   **Railroad:** NH   **Length:** 11.2   **Opened:** 1877
The Rhode Island & Massachusetts RR constructed this segment as part of its line between Franklin and Valley Falls. The New York & New England RR, which took over operation as soon as it was completed as its Valley Falls Branch, used it to provide Boston-to-Providence passenger service. After the NH assumed control in 1898, however, through service was reduced. Passenger service was eliminated in 1930, and local traffic was light. The rails were removed in 1942. A gas pipeline uses the right of way.

155

Berlin, CT [2100 ft E]   East Berlin, CT [1000 ft W]
Abandoned: 1940   **Railroad:** NH   **Length:** 3.6   **Opened:** 1849
This segment formed part of the Middletown branch of the Hartford & New Haven RR. It became a branch of the NH in 1872. Between 1906 and the 1920s the line was electrified. Once the wires were removed, conventional passenger service continued until around 1932.

156

Canaan, CT [3770 ft E]   East Canaan, CT [2550 ft E]
Abandoned: 1940   **Railroad:** NH   **Length:** 2.3   **Opened:** 1871
Built by the Connecticut Western RR as part of its main line from Hartford to the Hudson, this became the Central New England RR in 1898. In 1927 it was taken over by the New Haven, who discontinued passenger service. This segment, which served one shipper, was abandoned so that the state of Connecticut could eliminate an underpass on U.S. Route 44.

157

Asylum St. Sta (Hartford), CT   State St. Sta (Hartford), CT
Abandoned: 1940   **Railroad:** NH   **Length:** 0.6   **Opened:** 1873
The Connecticut Valley RR built this extension of its main line from its terminus at the NH RR station at State St. to the Hartford, Providence & Fishkill RR station at Asylum St. It served little purpose once passenger service ended in 1931.

158

Hobarts, CT   Brookfield Jct., CT
Abandoned: 1940   **Railroad:** NH   **Length:** 2.2   **Opened:** 1840
This segment once formed the Bridgeport-Pittsfield main line of the Housantonic RR. The Housatonic operated independently until 1892 when it was absorbed by the NH. Passenger service ceased in 1932 and remaining Bridgeport-Pittsfield trains were re-routed by way of Norwalk and Danbury. Regular freight service ended in 1934.

159

South Easton, MA   Eastondale, MA
Abandoned: 1940   **Railroad:** NH   **Length:** 0.6   **Opened:** 1888
The Old Colony built this segment as part of its West Bridgewater Branch. It passed to the NH in 1893. Passenger service ceased in 1925, and the line was last used in 1937.

160

Bridgton Jct., ME   Bridgton, ME
Abandoned: 1941   **Railroad:** B&H   **Length:** 15.9   **Opened:** 1883
This line once formed part of the two-foot gauge Bridgton & Saco River RR. Its primary traffic was lumber. It was reorganized as the Bridgton & Harrison RR in 1928.

161

Forest Lake (Palmer), MA   Creamery (Hardwick), MA
Abandoned: 1941   **Railroad:** B&M   **Length:** 10.5   **Opened:** 1887
This was constructed between 1878 and 1887 as part of the Boston- to-Northampton main line of the Massachusetts Central (later Central Massachusetts) RR. It was operated for a few years by the Boston & Lowell RR before becoming part of the B&M in 1887. Passenger service ended in 1932. The line was taken out of service in January 1933, except for 2 miles between Creamery and Gilbertville. This was operated until September 1938 when floods caused by the great hurricane shut down the line.

162

Georgetown, MA   Paper Mill, MA
Abandoned: 1942   **Railroad:** B&M   **Length:** 4.5   **Opened:** 1851
The Newburyport RR built this branch from Georgetown to Bradford. It became part of the B&M in 1860. Passenger trains last ran in 1933. In 1936 a bridge in poor condition caused service to be suspended between Groveland and Paper Mill. Groveland continued to be served via Georgetown until abandonment.

163

Jewett, ME   Foundry (Somersworth), NH
Abandoned: 1942   **Railroad:** B&M   **Length:** 5.2   **Opened:** 1872
This line once formed part of the Great Falls & South Berwick RR. It completed tracks between its namesake points in 1855, but was not operated 1858-60. A new railroad, the Portsmouth, Great Falls, & Conway, took over the line in 1865. The Eastern RR absorbed the line in 1871 and completed this segment. In 1884 the B&M acquired it. Scheduled passenger service ended in 1936, although occasional excursion trains continued. By the time of abandonment only a single customer was left on the line.

164

Norwotuck (Amherst), MA   Canal Jct. (Belchertown), MA
Abandoned: 1942   **Railroad:** B&M   **Length:** 8.5   **Opened:** 1887
This was constructed between 1878 and 1887 as part of the Boston- to-Northampton main line of the Massachusetts Central (later Central Massachusetts) RR. It was operated for a few years by the Boston & Lowell RR before becoming part of the B&M in 1887. Passenger service ended in 1932 and the line was taken out of service, the B&M having acquired trackage rights over a parallel line of the B&A and CV.

165

Sawyers, NH   Dover Point, NH
Abandoned: 1941   **Railroad:** B&M   **Length:** 3.3   **Opened:** 1874
The Eastern RR leased the Portsmouth & Dover RR as soon as the latter had completed its 11-mile line between its namesake cities in 1874. The B&M took over a decade later. Passenger service ended in January 1933. This part of the old Portsmouth & Dover was taken out of service in 1936, except for 0.6 mile at Sawyer which was used until March 1938.

166

Squannacook Jct., MA   Pepperell, MA
Abandoned: 1942   **Railroad:** B&M   **Length:** 6.4   **Opened:** 1892
The Brookline & Pepperell built this line as part of a through line that eventually extended from Squannacook Jct. to Milford, NH. The Fitchburg RR leased the line when it opened. The B&M took over in 1900 and operated this as its Milford Branch. Passenger service ceased in 1931. At the time of abandonment the only remaining customers on the line were two paper companies in Pepperell. The B&M constructed a connection between its Worcester, Nashua & Rochester line to serve the mills. A short stretch of track in front of the Pepperell depot survived as a wye until 1983. Today the right of way in Pepperell is owned by a power company, but the line in Groton has reverted to private owners and has been built upon in places.

167

Topsfield, MA   Newburyport, MA
Abandoned: 1941   **Railroad:** B&M   **Length:** 15.5   **Opened:** 1854
The Newburyport RR opened its line between Newburyport and Georgetown in 1850. The Danvers & Georgetown RR extended this line to Danvers in 1854 (and another company continued the railroad to Wakefield Jct. where it connected with the B&M). The Newburyport operated the Danvers & Georgetown upon its completion, and used it to run trains over the B&M to Boston in competition with the Eastern RR. The B&M took over the Newburyport in 1860. Some freight and passenger service continued until abandonment.

168

Derby Jct., CT   Orange, CT
Abandoned: 1941   **Railroad:** NH   **Length:** 3.4   **Opened:** 1871
The New Haven & Derby RR constructed this segment as part of its New Haven-Derby-Ansonia line. Passenger trains stopped running in 1925. The tracks were removed in 1942.

170

Dover, NH [0.5 mi N]   Gonic, NH
Abandoned: 1943   **Railroad:** B&M   **Length:** 7   **Opened:** 1849
The Cocheco RR opened this segment as part of its line from Dover to Alton Bay, which it reached in 1851. It passed to the B&M in 1863. Passenger service ended in 1935.

171

Farmington, NH   Alton, NH
Abandoned: 1942   **Railroad:** B&M   **Length:** 9.1   **Opened:** 1851
Part of the same route as line 170; see the note for that segment.

172

Franklin Jct., NH   Franklin Falls, NH
Abandoned: 1942   **Railroad:** B&M   **Length:** 1.1   **Opened:** 1892
The Franklin & Tilton RR constructed this segment as part of its line between Franklin Jct. and Tilton. It was leased on completion to the Concord & Montreal RR and in 1895 passed to the B&M. Passenger service ended in the 1920s. Damage from floods took it out of service in 1936.

173

Hamilton & Wenham, MA [2000 ft E]   Essex, MA
Abandoned: 1942   **Railroad:** B&M   **Length:** 5.5   **Opened:** 1872
The Eastern RR constructed this line as its Essex Branch. Traffic included lumber for shipyards at Essex and picnickers bound for Centennial Grove on Chebacco Lake. The B&M attempted unsuccessfully to abandon this line as early as 1926. With the decline of shipbuilding that accompanied the Great Depression, and the end of ice production on Chebacco Lake, traffic declined and the B&M sought once more to have the line abandoned in August 1942. Emphasizing the scrap value that the rails would have toward the war effort, the I.C.C. brushed aside objections from residents and the state and permitted the abandonment in November 1942. The rails were gone by the year's end.

174

Hillsboro, NH   Emerson, NH
Abandoned: 1942   **Railroad:** B&M   **Length:** 4.6   **Opened:** 1849
Built as part of the Contoocook Valley RR (Contoocook-Hillsboro), this line was operated by various railroads until 1873 when it became part of the Concord & Claremont RR, which subsequently became part of the Boston & Lowell (1884) and B&M (1887). Passenger service ended around 1936.

175

Hollis, NH   Nashua, NH [1 mi SW of Union Sta.]
Abandoned: 1942   **Railroad:** B&M   **Length:** 4.6   **Opened:** 1848
The Worcester & Nashua RR constructed this line between its namesake cities in 1848. Eventually the line was extended to Rochester, NH., and ultimately to Portland. Renamed the Worcester, Nashua, & Rochester RR in 1883, it became part of the B&M 3 years later. For a time this was a busy main line, but eventually most traffic was routed over other lines. Passenger and freight service ended in 1934. The line was last used in March 1936 when floods closed the Nashua & Lowell line into Nashua.

176

Lakeport, NH   Lily Pond, NH
Abandoned: ca. 1942   **Railroad:** B&M   **Length:** 3   **Opened:** 1890
Built by the Lake Shore RR and controlled by the Concord & Montreal RR, this line became part of the B&M in 1895. It once carried substantial numbers of passengers to Lake Winnipesaukee summer resorts, but by the late 1930s it saw few passengers. Passenger trains were last operated in 1935. The track remained in place until the 1950s. One mile of track at Lakeport was retained as an industrial spur.

177

Nashua, NH   Hudson, NH
Abandoned: 1942   **Railroad:** B&M   **Length:** 4   **Opened:** 1874
The Nashua & Rochester RR built this line as an extension of the Worcester & Nashua RR. After the B&M acquired it in 1886, it formed part of its Worcester, Nashua & Rochester division, a through route between Worcester and Rochester. Service on the line ended in March 1934.

178

Peterboro, NH   Elmwood, NH
Abandoned: 1942   **Railroad:** B&M   **Length:** 6.5   **Opened:** 1878
The Peterboro & Hillsboro RR built this line, but it was controlled by the Northern RR. It became a B&M branch in 1889. Passenger service ceased around 1936.

179

South Milford, NH   Milford, NH
Abandoned: 1942   **Railroad:** B&M   **Length:** 1.5   **Opened:** 1895
The Brookline & Milford RR built this branch for the Fitchburg RR as an extension of existing lines from Squannacook Jct. to Brookline. The B&M assumed control in 1900. Passenger trains last used the line in 1931.

179A

Orono, ME   Stillwater, ME
Abandoned: ca. 1942   **Railroad:** MC   **Length:** 3   **Opened:** 1890
The MC built this branch around 1890. It was apparently used only for freight service.

180

Bellingham Jct., MA   Caryville, MA
Abandoned: 1941   **Railroad:** NH   **Length:** 2.9   **Opened:** 1863
The New York & Boston RR produced this segment as part of its main line between Brookline, Mass., and Woonsocket, RI. Eventually the line passed to the New York & New England RR and in 1898, the NH. Passenger service on the line, which consisted of commuter trains to Boston, was suspended in 1938 but restored in 1940 and continued until abandonment. The I.C.C. authorized the NH to abandon 4.1 miles between Bellingham Jct. and West Medway but the segment between Caryville and West Medway remained in use for freight for another eight years (see line 193A).

180A

at Rockport, ME
Abandoned: 1942   **Railroad:** LR   **Length:** 9   **Opened:** 1889
Although the LR reported as a common carrier, this freight-only line was basically an industrial railroad serving lime quarries near Rockport.

182

Hooksett, NH   Suncook, NH [2200 ft S of SV Jct.]
Abandoned: 1943   **Railroad:** B&M   **Length:** 1.3   **Opened:** 1869
The Concord RR built this line as part of a connection to the Suncook Valley RR. It became part of the Concord & Montreal RR in 1889, and joined the B&M in 1895.

183

Maynard, MA   Central Mass. Jct. (Hudson), MA
Abandoned: 1943   **Railroad:** B&M   **Length:** 4.5   **Opened:** 1850
The Fitchburg RR used a charter obtained for the Lancaster & Sterling RR to build this line as part of its Marlboro Branch. The B&M assumed control in 1900. Passenger trains last operated here in 1932.

184

Northampton, MA [3662 ft N]   Cheapside (Deerfield), MA
Abandoned: 1943   **Railroad:** NH   **Length:** 17.1   **Opened:** 1882
The New Haven & Northampton RR extended its main line from Northampton to Shelburne Jct. in 1881 in hopes of capturing traffic using the newly opened Hoosac Tunnel. These hopes were never realized. This section was closely paralleled by the Connecticut River line of the B&M. Passenger service ended around 1919, but the line somehow hung on until World War II.

185

North Berwick, ME   Biddeford, ME
Abandoned: 1944   **Railroad:** B&M   **Length:** 17.9   **Opened:** 1842
Built by the Portland, Saco & Portsmouth RR, this formed part of the original main line between Boston and Portland. Between 1847 and 1870 it was jointly leased by the rival Eastern & B&M. When the Eastern gained sole control of the line in 1870 (at great expense), the B&M constructed the line to Portland that Guilford trains still use today. The old PS&P line became part of the B&M in 1884, and the B&M continued to operate two parallel routes between Boston and Portland until the 1940s. Passenger service, however, ended around 1926.

186

Saco, ME   Rigby (Scarboro), ME
Abandoned: 1944   **Railroad:** B&M   **Length:** 9.7   **Opened:** 1842
Built by the Portland, Saco & Portsmouth RR, this formed part of the original main line between Boston and Portland. Between 1847 and 1870 it was jointly leased by the rival Eastern & B&M. When the Eastern gained sole control of the line in 1870 (at great expense) the B&M constructed the line to Portland that Guilford trains still use today. This line became part of the B&M in 1884, and the the B&M continued to operate two parallel

routes between Boston and Portland until the 1940s. Passenger service, however, ended around 1926.

187

Monson Jct., ME   Monson Slate Quarries, ME
Abandoned: 1944   **Railroad:** MON   **Length:** 8.2   **Opened:** 1883
The last of the Maine two-gauge railroads to operate, the Monson differed from most other such lines in that slate, not timber, was the primary commodity it carried. Passenger service ended in 1938, and by 1943 it had ceased operating.

187A

Willows, MA   Ayer, MA
Abandoned: 1946   **Railroad:** B&M   **Length:** 2.3   **Opened:** 1848
When the Stony Brook RR opened its line from Lowell (North Chelmsford) to Ayer in 1848, it closely paralleled 2 miles of the main line of the Fitchburg RR. The Stony Brook became a branch of the Nashua & Lowell RR and later the Boston & Lowell RR. By 1900 both it and the former Fitchburg RR were components of the B&M system. In 1946 the B&M built a connection between the Stony Brook and the Fitchburg at Willows and abandoned the original Stony Brook line into Ayer.

188

River Bank (Montague), MA   Turners Falls, MA
Abandoned: 1947   **Railroad:** B&M   **Length:** 1.5   **Opened:** 1868
The Vermont & Massachusetts RR constructed this branch into Turners Falls. The Fitchburg RR assumed control in 1874, and was in turn absorbed by the B&M in 1900. Passenger service ended in 1913. The great floods of March 1936 destroyed a bridge and took the line out of service. The B&M at this time acquired trackage rights over a parallel NH branch. When the B&M bought the latter branch from the NH it was permitted to abandon this long unused line.

189

Pittsfield, NH   Center Barnstead, NH
Abandoned: 1947   **Railroad:** SV   **Length:** 4.6   **Opened:** 1889
The Suncook Valley Extension RR was the name under which the Concord & Montreal RR extended its branch line to Center Barnstead. The B&M took over in 1895. In 1923 the B&M returned the Suncook Valley RR, which had been operated under lease since 1869, back to independent operation, along with the extension. Passenger service was discontinued around 1942.

190

Hope Valley, RI   Wood River Jct., RI
Abandoned: 1947   **Railroad:** WRB   **Length:** 5.7   **Opened:** 1874
The WRB operated as an independent short line for most of its existence. Passenger service ended in 1927. It could not survive the destruction by fire of its largest customer—a feed and grain mill in Hope Valley, whose owner also owned the railroad—in March 1947.

191

Coos Jct., NH   North Stratford, NH
Abandoned: 1948   **Railroad:** MC   **Length:** 19.4   **Opened:** 1891
This line was built as part of the Upper Coos RR, which ran from Quebec Jct., NH, to Paquetteville, PQ. It was leased to the MC. Passenger service ended around 1938.

192

Hawleyville, CT   Litchfield, CT
Abandoned: 1948   **Railroad:** NH   **Length:** 32.4   **Opened:** 1872
This line was built as the Shepaug Valley RR. After several years as an independent short line (under 3 names in all) it became a branch of the NH in 1898. Passenger service ended in 1930.

193

Hawleyville, CT   Southbury, CT
Abandoned: 1948   **Railroad:** NH   **Length:** 9.1   **Opened:** 1881
It took the New York & New England RR 15 years to construct its extension from Waterbury to Brewster and Poughkeepsie, NY., of which this segment formed part. In 1898 it passed to the NH, which had little need for the section east of Danbury. Passenger trains stopped running in 1932.

193A

Caryville, MA   West Medway, MA
Abandoned: 1949   **Railroad:** NH   **Length:** 1.2   **Opened:** 1863
The New York & Boston RR produced this segment as part of its main line between Brookline, Mass., and Woonsocket, RI. Eventually the line passed to the New York & New England RR and in 1898, the NH. Passenger service on the line, which consisted of commuter trains to Boston, was suspended in 1938 but restored in 1940 and continued until 1941. The I.C.C. authorized the NH to abandon this segment in 1941, but abandonment did not take place until 8 years later (see line 180).

194

South Barre, VT   Barre, VT
Abandoned: 1950   **Railroad:** CV   **Length:** 2.7   **Opened:** 1888
The CV constructed this line as an extension of its Barre Branch. Passenger service ended in 1938.

195

Arkright, RI   Hope, RI
Abandoned: 1951   **Railroad:** NH   **Length:** 1   **Opened:** 1874
The Pawtuxet Valley RR built this line under the auspices of the Hartford, Providence & Fishkill RR, which operated the line upon completion. It later was expanded and transferred to the New York & New England RR, the New York, Providence & Boston, and finally, in 1892, to the NH. Passenger service ended around 1926.

196

Whiting, VT   Larrabees Point, VT
Abandoned: 1951   **Railroad:** RUT   **Length:** 10.4   **Opened:** 1871
This once formed part of the Addison RR, built in hopes of opening a new route between New England and the West across Lake Champlain. Before completion it was leased by the Rutland, and it was always operated as a Rutland branch. Unfortunately, the anticipated traffic never materialized.

196A

Hills Crossing, MA   Clematis Brook, MA
Abandoned: 1952   **Railroad:** B&M   **Length:** 3   **Opened:** 1881
This was part of the original main line of the Massachusetts Central (later Central Massachusetts) RR, which ran from Boston to Northampton. The Boston & Lowell operated this for a few years before it became a B&M branch. This segment was closely paralleled by the main line of the Fitchburg RR, which the B&M also acquired in 1900.

197

Kittery (Navy Yard), ME   North Berwick, ME
Abandoned: 1952   **Railroad:** B&M   **Length:** 16.7   **Opened:** 1842
Built by the Portland, Saco & Portsmouth RR, this formed part of the original main line between Boston and Portland. Between 1847 and 1870 it was jointly leased by the rival Eastern & B&M. When the Eastern gained sole control of the line in 1870 (at great expense), the B&M constructed the line to Portland that Guilford trains still use today. The old PS&P became part of the B&M in 1884, and the B&M continued to operate two parallel routes between Boston and Portland until the 1940s. Today most of the right of way carries a gas pipeline.

198

Rumford Jct. (Auburn), ME   Canton, ME
Abandoned: 1952   **Railroad:** MC   **Length:** 35.9   **Opened:** 1893
The broad-gauge Buckfield Branch RR built a line from Mechanics Falls to Buckfield in 1849. This railroad was sold to the Portland & Oxford Central RR in 1857 and extended to Canton in 1870. It was operated only sporadically until 1874, when the Rumford Falls & Buckfield RR took over. The latter company reopened the line and converted it to standard gauge in 1878. In 1890 it became the Portland & Rumford Falls RR and in 1893 was extended to Rumford Jct. The MC absorbed the latter company in 1907. Passenger service continued until shortly before the line was abandoned altogether.

199

Atlantic, MA   West Quincy, MA
Abandoned: 1952   **Railroad:** NH   **Length:** 3.1   **Opened:** 1871
The Old Colony RR constructed this branch, which ultimately ran from Atlantic to Braintree. It incorporated part of the right of way of the old Granite RR, which opened in 1826. Passenger service ended in 1940 and the following year the tracks between Atlantic and East Milton were taken out of service.

200

Springvale, ME   Rochester, NH
Abandoned: 1952   **Railroad:** S&E   **Length:** 15.6   **Opened:** 1871
The Portland & Rochester RR constructed this line as part of its main line. It became part of the B&M in 1884 and formed part of a through route between Portland and Worcester, MA. Passenger service continued until the early 1930s. The B&M sold this line to the new Sanford & Eastern RR in 1949, but the short line soon found it could not afford to operate it.

202

Rodmans Crossing (Wakefield), RI   Narragansett Pier, RI
Abandoned: 1953   **Railroad:** NP   **Length:** 2.3   **Opened:** 1876
The NP was a short line to the resort community of Narragansett Pier. When passenger service on the NP ended in 1952, there was little demand for this part of the line. The state requested abandonment to save it the expense of building a highway overpass, and the railroad obliged.

203

North Milford, MA   Hopkinton, MA
Abandoned: 1953   **Railroad:** NH   **Length:** 3   **Opened:** 1872
The Hopkinton RR opened this railroad as part of its line from Ashland to Milford. On completion it was leased first to the Providence & Worcester RR, and in 1883 it became part of the Milford & Woonsocket RR. Four years later it was absorbed by the New York & New England RR and in 1898 it became a branch of the NH. Passenger service ended in 1920. In 1953 the I.C.C. authorized abandonment of the line all the way to Milford, but the NH continued to operate the 3.1-mile segment between Milford and North Milford.

204

Tremont, MA [2.1 mi S]   Fairhaven, MA
Abandoned: 1953   **Railroad:** NH   **Length:** 12.8   **Opened:** 1854
Built by the Fairhaven Branch RR, this line was operated by the New Bedford & Taunton RR, with which it did not directly connect. It became part of the Old Colony RR in 1879 and the NH in 1893. Passenger service ended in 1938. At the time of abandonment the initial 2 miles were reclassified as an industrial spur serving the Marion sand pit. That segment continued in operation until 1976; the tracks remain in place.

204A

Bennington, VT   Peterburgh Jct., NY
Abandoned: 1953   **Railroad:** RUT   **Length:** 11.7   **Opened:** 1869
The Lebanon Springs RR constructed this line as part of it its route to Chatham, NY. Shortly after it opened it was taken over by the Harlem Extension RR and in 1873 by the Vermont Central (later the Central Vermont). The Rutland acquired the line in 1901. Passenger service continued until around 1938.

204B

West Quincy, MA   Granite, MA
Abandoned: 1953   **Railroad:** NH   **Length:** 0.5   **Opened:** 1873
The Old Colony RR constructed this branch, which ultimately ran from Atlantic to Braintree. It incorporated part of the right of way of the old Granite RR, which opened in 1826. Passenger service ended in 1940. The Southeast Expressway uses part of this right of way.

205

Bow Jct., NH   Suncook, NH   Pittsfield, NH
Abandoned: 1953   **Railroad:** SV   **Length:** 22.9   **Opened:** 1869
In 1869 the Suncook Valley RR opened its line between Suncook and Pittsfield. It was leased and operated by the Concord RR, and in 1895 it became a branch of the B&M. The line between Bow Jct. and Suncook had been built as a branch of the Concord in the 1860s. In 1923 the B&M returned the Suncook Valley RR back to independent operation. The line never enjoyed great success. By the early 1950s the Suncook Valley's finances had become so precarious that creditors threatened to take possession of the railroad's only locomotive. With traffic light there was no option but abandonment.

206

Plymouth, NH   Blackmount, NH
Abandoned: 1954   **Railroad:** B&M   **Length:** 37   **Opened:** 1853
The Boston, Concord & Montreal RR opened the section between Plymouth and Warren in 1851 and completed the line through Blackmount in 1853. The BC&M stretched 94 miles from Concord, NH, to Wells River, VT, and for many years formed part of a major through route between Boston and Canada. After 1889 this was part of the Concord & Montreal RR and in 1895, the B&M. Passenger service continued until abandonment, which was marked by protests from the communities, passengers, and shippers affected.

206A

Lakewood, RI   Bellefonte, RI
Abandoned: 1954   **Railroad:** WARW   **Length:** 1   **Opened:** 1875
The Warwick RR opened an 8-mile line from Cranston to Oakland Beach in 1875. In 1879 it was reorganized as the Rhode Island Central RR, under the control of the New York, Providence & Boston RR. The NH took over the line in 1893, but in 1900 transferred it to its subsidiary, the Rhode Island Suburban RY, which converted it into a trolley line. The Rhode Island Suburban company became the United Electric Railways in 1921. Passenger service ended in 1935, but electric freight service continued. In 1936 the line beyond Lakewood was abandoned. United Electric in 1949 sold the line to a new Warwick RY, which converted the railroad to diesel operation in 1952.

207

Easton, MA   South Easton, MA
Abandoned: 1954   **Railroad:** NH   **Length:** 1.1   **Opened:** 1888
This line formed part of the Old Colony RR's West Bridgewater Branch. It became part of the NH in 1893. Passenger service came to an end in 1925.

207A

Stevens, MA   Machine Shop, MA
Abandoned: ca. 1955   **Railroad:** B&M   **Length:** 1   **Opened:** 1848
This was a short remnant of the main line of the Essex RR between Salem and Lawrence, operated first by the Eastern RR and after 1884 by the B&M. Passenger service was discontinued in 1926, when most of the old Essex RR was abandoned.

208

Montpelier, VT   Wells River, VT
Abandoned: 1956   **Railroad:** B&C   **Length:** 37.9   **Opened:** 1873
The Montpelier & Wells River RR constructed this line. It was operated more or less independently for many years until becoming part of the Barre & Chelsea RR in 1944. Today 13 miles of the right of way through Groton State Forest form the Montpelier and Wells River Trail.

209

East Swanton, VT   Canadian border
Abandoned: 1956   **Railroad:** CV   **Length:** 8   **Opened:** 1889
This branch of the CV originally formed part of its East Alburgh extension from East Swanton to St. Johns, PQ. Passenger service ended in 1946. The Canadian section (operated by the Grand Trunk and later the CN) to St. Johns had been abandoned in 1952.

210

Collinsville, CT   New Hartford, CT
Abandoned: 1956   **Railroad:** NH   **Length:** 6.2   **Opened:** 1876
The New Haven & Northampton RR had opened an 8-mile branch from Farmington, CT, to Collinsville, CT, in 1850, at the time its main line was constructed. In 1870 the line was extended another 5 miles to Pine Meadow, and 1876 another mile to New Hartford. The branch passed to the NH in 1887. Passenger service lasted until around 1928.

211

Granite, MA   Washington St. (West Quincy), MA
Abandoned: 1956   **Railroad:** NH   **Length:** 0.6   **Opened:** 1873
The Old Colony RR constructed this segment, part of a branch which ran from Atlantic to Braintree. Passenger service ended in 1940. The route of the new Southeast Expressway used this right of way, which was the reason for abandonment.

211A

Lakewood, RI   Bellefonte, RI
Abandoned: 1956   **Railroad:** WARW   **Length:** 0.5   **Opened:** 1875
The original Warwick RR was an unsuccessful short line railroad that opened its 8-mile route from Cranston to Oakland Beach in 1875. Reorganized after failure in 1879, it became the Rhode Island Central RR and became a branch of the New York, Providence & Boston RR. The NH took over in 1892. In 1899 the NH transferred the line to a subsidiary trolley company, the Rhode Island Suburban RY (later, United Electric), which electrified the route. Trolleys used the route until 1935, and electric freight continued

until 1952 when they gave way to diesels. By this time the old trolley company had sold the line to a new Warwick RY, which had no use for this segment by 1956.

212

East Winsted, CT   West Winsted, CT
Abandoned: 1957   **Railroad:** NH   **Length:** 0.8   **Opened:** 1871
Built by the Connecticut Western RR as part of its main line from Hartford to the Hudson River, this eventually became the Central New England RR in 1898. It became part of the New Haven in 1927, at which time passenger service was discontinued. This segment had been out of service since 1955 due to flood damage.

213

Brookline Jct., MA   Riverside, MA
Abandoned: 1958   **Railroad:** B&A   **Length:** 10   **Opened:** 1886
The Boston & Worcester RR opened its three-mile Brookline Branch in 1848, and the Charles River RR extended it to Newton Highlands in 1852. The New York & New England RR, which succeeded the Charles River, sold its part of this line to the Boston & Albany (successor to the Boston & Worcester) in 1883. The B&A constructed a short connecting line from Riverside to Newton Highlands in 1886, which gave it a loop line that paralleled its own main line between Brookline Jct. and Riverside. The Highland Circuit, as it became known, remained a busy commuter line until abandonment, which enabled the Metropolitan Transit Authority to convert the branch into a trolley route. The new line opened in 1959, and today continues as the MBTA's Riverside line (Green Line).

214

Webster Jct., MA   Webster, MA
Abandoned: 1958   **Railroad:** B&A   **Length:** 11   **Opened:** 1884
The Providence, Webster & Springfield RR built this branch in 1884 to give Webster an additional rail outlet. The B&A operated the line, although it never owned it. Passenger service ended around 1919. Abandonment was caused by the construction of a flood control project that would have flooded part of the line. A short section in Webster remained in service until 1971 as an industrial spur connected to the New Haven's Norwich & Worcester line.

215

Webster Mills, MA   East Village, MA
Abandoned: 1958   **Railroad:** B&A   **Length:** 1.3   **Opened:** 1884
The Providence, Webster & Springfield RR built this short branch in 1884 at the same time as its main line (see line 214). The B&A operated the line, although it never owned it. This was apparently only operated for freight, its primary customer being the Slater Mill in East Village. Abandonment of the main line, necessitated by a flood control project, led to the abandonment of this line at the same time.

216

Berlin, MA   Clinton Jct. (Clinton), MA
Abandoned: 1958   **Railroad:** B&M   **Length:** 5.6   **Opened:** 1903
The portion of this abandonment between Berlin and West Berlin formed part of the original main line of the Massachusetts Central (later Central Massachusetts) RR, which

extended from Boston to Northampton. That section opened in 1882, was closed for two years, and eventually wound up as a subsidiary of the Boston & Lowell RR. The B&M took over in 1887. In 1903 the construction of the Wachusett Reservoir caused the B&M to abandon the original Central Mass mainline between West Berlin and Oakdale (see line 15A) and construct a new line between West Berlin and Clinton Jct., where connection was made with the B&M's Worcester, Nashua & Rochester Division. Passenger service ended in 1958, and the line was abandoned some months later. The abandoned line included a viaduct and a tunnel under part of Clinton; the tunnel still exists.

216A

Montpelier Jct., VT   Barre, VT
Abandoned: 1958   **Railroad:** M&B   **Length:** 6   **Opened:** 1889
In 1958 the Montpelier & Barre RR acquired the CV branch from Montpelier Jct. to Barre that closely paralleled its own main line between those points. The M&B main line had been formerly that of the Barre & Chelsea RR. It had been built in 2 sections. The first, from Montpelier Jct. to Barre Transfer, was completed by the Montpelier & Wells River RR in 1873; the rest of the line to Barre was opened by the Barre RR in 1889. The CV line had been completed in 1876 by the Montpelier & White River RR, which reached 15 miles from Montpelier Jct. to Williamstown. The line was taken over upon completion by the CV. Passenger service on the Barre & Chelsea ended in 1922 and was discontinued on the CV line in 1939. Upon obtaining the CV branch, the M&B abandoned it from Route 302 to Barre, and discontinued its own main line between Route 302 and Montpelier Jct.

217

Waterbury, CT   East Farms, CT
Abandoned: 1958   **Railroad:** NH   **Length:** 1.3   **Opened:** 1888
Built as part of the Meriden, Waterbury & Connecticut RR, this line became part of the New York & New England in 1892. Not operated between 1896 and 1898, it became a seldom-used line of the New Haven. Passenger service ended in 1917. The construction of Interstate-84 led to the abandonment of this segment.

218

Heywood (Gardner), MA   Winchendon, MA
Abandoned: 1959   **Railroad:** B&M   **Length:** 7.6   **Opened:** 1874
The Boston, Barre & Gardner RR built this line as part of its main line between Worcester and Winchenden. Passenger service ceased in 1953. At the time of abandonment it was out of service.

218A

Medford, MA   Park St. (Medford), MA
Abandoned: 1959   **Railroad:** B&M   **Length:** 0.5   **Opened:** 1847
The B&M built its two-mile Medford Branch in 1847, two years after it opened its Wilmington Jct.-Boston main line. Once passenger service to Medford ended in 1957, there was no further use for the outermost half-mile of the branch.

219

Waukeag, ME   Washington Jct., ME
Abandoned: 1959   **Railroad:** MC   **Length:** 8   **Opened:** 1884
The Maine Shore Line RR built this line for the MC, and on completion the line was taken over by the MC. It provided access to the wharves where ferries operated to Bar Harbor on Mount Desert Island. The ferry was discontinued in April 1931, leaving only mixed train service on the branch, which ended two years later. This portion survived as a local freight branch until abandonment.

220

Putnam, CT   Pomfret, CT
Abandoned: 1959   **Railroad:** NH   **Length:** 4.3   **Opened:** 1872
The Boston, Hartford & Erie RR opened this segment in 1872 as part of its Boston-to-Hartford main line. It became a component of the New York & New England RR in 1875 and ultimately part of the NH in 1898. Daily Boston-Hartford passenger trains used the route until August 1955 when severe floods destroyed a bridge near Putnam and took the line out of service. This segment never reopened.

220A

Fells Ave. (Milford), MA   North Milford, MA
Abandoned: 1959   **Railroad:** NH   **Length:** 3.1   **Opened:** 1872
The Hopkinton RR opened this railroad as part of its line from Ashland to Milford. On completion it was leased first to the Providence & Worcester RR, and in 1883 it became part of the Milford & Woonsocket RR. Four years later it was absorbed by the New York & New England RR and in 1898 it became a branch of the NH. Passenger service ended in 1920. In 1953 the I.C.C. authorized abandonment of the line (see line 203), but the NH continued to operate it until 1959.

221

Union Market (Watertown), MA [W of sta.]   Bemis, MA
Abandoned: 1960   **Railroad:** B&M   **Length:** 0.9   **Opened:** 1849
The Watertown Branch was built by the Fitchburg RR, and one time carried a heavy load of commuters. Traffic was so heavy that in 1893 it became one of the few branch lines to be double tracked. The B&M took over in 1900. Passenger service was finally eliminated in 1938. This abandonment, which divided the Watertown line into 2 separate branches, was done so that the grade crossing in busy Watertown Square could be eliminated.

221B

Gonic, NH   Rochester, NH
Abandoned: ca. 1960   **Railroad:** B&M   **Length:** 2   **Opened:** 1874
The Nashua & Rochester RR built this line as part of its extension of the Worcester & Nashua RR. After the B&M acquired it in 1886 it formed part of its Worcester, Nashua & Rochester division, a through route between Worcester and Rochester. Originally this segment was closely paralleled by the Lake Shore (Cocheco) line (Dover-Alton Bay), both routes entering Rochester together. After the building of the Spaulding Turnpike around 1955, the B&M rerouted all traffic from this branch over the Lake Shore route, and a few years later it was removed.

222

Contoocook, NH   Garrison (West Concord), NH
Abandoned: 1960   **Railroad:** C&C   **Length:** 9.1   **Opened:** 1849
The Concord & Claremont RR built this line. It was merged with other lines to form the New Hampshire Central RR in 1853. It became the C&C once more in 1873, but eventually passed to the B&M in 1887. In 1954 the B&M sold the line to a new Claremont & Concord RR. Passenger service ended the year following. The line was out of service at the time of abandonment due to a damaged trestle.

223

West Hopkinton, NH   Emerson, NH
Abandoned: 1960   **Railroad:** C&C   **Length:** 6.7   **Opened:** 1849
Built as part of the Contoocook Valley RR (Contoocook-Hillsboro), this line was operated by various railroads until 1873 when it became part of the Concord & Claremont RR, which subsequently became part of the Boston & Lowell (1884) and B&M (1887). Passenger service ended around 1936. The B&M sold the line to a new Claremont & Concord RR in 1954. This segment was abandoned because of a flood control project that took part of the right of way.

223A

Neponset, MA   Atlantic, MA
Abandoned: 1960   **Railroad:** NH   **Length:** 0.5   **Opened:** 1845
This formed part of the original main line of the Old Colony RR from Boston to Plymouth. Most of this segment consisted of a bridge across the Neponset River and the approach tracks to it. As the Old Colony system expanded, it carried ever-increasing numbers of commuter trains in and out of Boston. After the NH absorbed the Old Colony in 1893 traffic continued to grow; by 1913 the line had been increased to 4 tracks. More than 100 trains a day crossed the bridge. In 1959, after many years of trying, the NH was permitted to abandon passenger service on the Old Colony lines. The following year, the bridge burned and the railroad saw no need to rebuild it. In 1971 the MBTA opened its Red Line rapid transit extension to Quincy along this route. Recently, the MBTA and the state of Massachusetts have rebuilt the bridge in order to restore passenger service on the Old Colony lines, and this segment should soon be back in service.

224

North Eastham, MA   Provincetown, MA
Abandoned: 1960   **Railroad:** NH   **Length:** 19.8   **Opened:** 1873
The Cape Cod Central RR built this line as an extension of the Cape Cod RR. The section between North Eastham and Wellfleet opened in 1871; the Old Colony RR took over and opened the line to Provincetown two years later. The line passed to the NH in 1893. Passenger service ended in 1938, although it was revived briefly in 1940.

225

Leicester Jct., VT   Whiting, VT
Abandoned: 1961   **Railroad:** RUT   **Length:** 3.1   **Opened:** 1871
This once formed part of the Addison RR, built in hopes of opening a new route between New England and the West across Lake Champlain. Before completion it was leased by the Rutland, and it was always operated as a Rutland branch. Unfortunately, the anticipated

traffic never materialized. By the time of abandonment, the line, which included 7 bridges, was said to be in very poor condition.

225A

Park St. (Medford), MA   Glenwood, MA
Abandoned: ca. 1961   **Railroad:** B&M   **Length:** 0.5   **Opened:** 1847
The B&M built its two-mile Medford Branch in 1847, two years after it opened its Wilmington Jct.-Boston main line. Passenger service on the branch ended in 1957.

226

Swampscott, MA   Marblehead, MA
Abandoned: 1961   **Railroad:** B&M   **Length:** 4   **Opened:** 1873
The Eastern RR built this, its Swampscott Branch, in 1873, just as that line slid into virtual bankruptcy. This was its second branch to Marblehead. It became a B&M branch in 1884. Passenger service survived until 1959.

227

Woburn, MA   North Woburn Jct., MA [S of Sta.]
Abandoned: 1961   **Railroad:** B&M   **Length:** 3.6   **Opened:** 1885
The Boston & Lowell RR built this line as an extension of its Woburn Branch so as to form a bypass of its main line. For many years certain Boston-Lowell trains were diverted to serve Woburn. Once passenger service ended in 1959, however, the line served little purpose and was abandoned.

228

West Hopkinton, NH   Bradford, NH
Abandoned: 1961   **Railroad:** C&C   **Length:** 17.6   **Opened:** 1850
Built by the original Concord & Claremont RR, this line was merged with other lines to form the New Hampshire Central RR in 1853. It became the C&C once more in 1873, but eventually passed to the B&M in 1887. In 1954 the B&M sold the line to a new Claremont & Concord RR. Passenger service ended the year following.

229

Newfield (Middletown), CT   East Berlin, CT
Abandoned: 1961   **Railroad:** NH   **Length:** 4.1   **Opened:** 1848
The Hartford & New Haven RR built this line as part of its Middletown Branch. It became part of the NH when that railroad was created in 1872. Between 1906 and the 1920s it was electrified with trolley wire. Passenger service finally ended around 1932.

230

West Stockbridge, MA   State Line, MA
Abandoned: 1961   **Railroad:** NH   **Length:** 2.6   **Opened:** 1843
This segment formed part of the State Line Branch of the Housatonic RR, which in fact had served as the original main line of that railroad for 7 years. The NH absorbed the Housatonic in 1892. Passenger service ended in 1928, but for many years the line carried through freight trains for interchange with the B&A at State Line. The line was last used for regular service in 1959.

231

Sanford, ME   Westbrook, ME
Abandoned: 1961   **Railroad:** S&E   **Length:** 31.8   **Opened:** 1871
The Portland & Rochester RR constructed this line as part of its main line. It became part of the B&M in 1884 and formed part of a through route between Portland and Worcester, MA. Passenger service continued until the early 1930s. The B&M sold this line to the new Sanford & Eastern RR in 1949,

232

Greenville, ME   Guilford Mill Yard, ME
Abandoned: 1962   **Railroad:** BAR   **Length:** 27   **Opened:** 1884
The Bangor & Piscataquis RR constructed this line as part of its broad gauge main line from Bangor to Greenville. The BAR bought the line in 1891. Passenger service lasted until 1958.

233

Bedford, MA   Concord, MA
Abandoned: 1962   **Railroad:** B&M   **Length:** 3.8   **Opened:** 1873
The Middlesex Central RR built this line for the Boston & Lowell RR to extend the latter's Lexington & Arlington Branch to Concord. This became a branch of the B&M in 1887. Passenger service ceased in 1926. Traffic in the line's final years was light indeed; it was said at abandonment that the line had seen only 19 carloads of freight in 19 years!

234

Bedford, MA   Billerica, MA
Abandoned: 1962   **Railroad:** B&M   **Length:** 5.3   **Opened:** 1885
The Boston & Lowell RR built this branch along much of the same right of way as that of the short-lived Billerica & Bedford narrow gauge line (1877-78; see line 9). The B&M took over the line shortly after its completion. At one time trains were run between Boston and Lowell using this route. Passenger service ceased in 1933.

235

Forest River (Salem), MA   Marblehead, MA
Abandoned: 1962   **Railroad:** B&M   **Length:** 1.4   **Opened:** 1839
The first of what later became 2 branch lines to Marblehead, this line was built along with the original Eastern RR from Boston to Newburyport. It became another B&M branch in 1884. Passenger trains continued until 1959.

235A

Peabody, MA   West Peabody, MA
Abandoned: 1962   **Railroad:** B&M   **Length:** 3   **Opened:** 1850
This was part of the Salem & Lowell RR's main line between its namesake cities. It was operated first by the Lowell & Lawrence RR and after 1858 by the Boston & Lowell. It became a branch of the B&M in 1887. Passenger service ended in 1932.

236

Florence, MA   Williamsburg, MA
Abandoned: 1962   **Railroad:** NH   **Length:** 4   **Opened:** 1868
The New Haven & Northampton RR built this line as part of its Williamsburg Branch (which connected to its main line in Northampton). The NH took control of the line in 1887 and ended passenger service around 1922.

237

Hingham, MA [1.1 mi E]   Greenbush, MA
Abandoned: 1962   **Railroad:** NH   **Length:** 9.7   **Opened:** 1871
The South Shore RR opened the portion of this line between Hingham and Cohasset in 1849. For a few years the Old Colony RR operated the line, but for more than 20 years the line ran independently. A second railroad, the Duxbury & Cohasset extended the line to Greenbush in 1871. By 1878 the Old Colony had taken over both lines. The Old Colony in turn was absorbed by the NH in 1893. Passenger service continued over this line until the discontinuation of all Old Colony commuter routes in 1959. Without passenger traffic there was little need for this line. Today the MBTA and the state are seeking to rebuild the line to reintroduce rail commuter service to Greenbush.

238

Olneyville, RI   Pascoag, RI
Abandoned: 1962   **Railroad:** NH   **Length:** 19.3   **Opened:** 1873
The Providence & Springfield built this line in hopes of opening a new route to the West from Providence, but the tracks never got beyond Douglas, MA. The New York & New England RR took over the line in 1890 and the NH assumed control in 1898. Passenger service ended around 1931.

239

Pratts Jct., MA   Sterling, MA
Abandoned: 1962   **Railroad:** NH   **Length:** 2.8   **Opened:** 1850
This line was constructed by the Fitchburg & Worcester RR as part of its main line. The Fitchburg & Worcester operated as an independent line until 1869 when it became part of the Boston, Clinton & Fitchburg RR. This system subsequently was acquired by the Old Colony RR in 1879 and the NH in 1893. Passenger service ended around 1926.

240

Wickford Jct., RI   Wickford, RI
Abandoned: 1962   **Railroad:** NH   **Length:** 2.5   **Opened:** 1871
The Newport & Wickford RR & Steamboat Co. opened this line as part of its branch to connect the New York, Boston & Providence RR with its steamboats on Narragansett Bay. The railroad continued to operate independently until World War I. Both steamboats and passenger trains ceased in October 1925.

241

Bradford, NH   Newport, NH
Abandoned: 1964   **Railroad:** C&C   **Length:** 16.2   **Opened:** 1871
The Sugar River RR built this line as an extension of the Concord & Claremont RR. It became part of the C&C in 1873, but eventually passed to the B&M in 1887. In 1954 the

B&M sold the line to a new Claremont & Concord RR. Passenger service ended the year following.

242

Branchville, CT   Ridgefield, CT

Abandoned: 1964   **Railroad:** NH   **Length:** 3.9   **Opened:** 1870

The Danbury & Norwalk RR constructed this short branch to Ridgefield. The Danbury & Norwalk became part of the Housatonic RR in 1886 and the NH in 1892. Passenger service on the branch ceased in 1925.

243

Ellington, CT   Westway, CT

Abandoned: 1964   **Railroad:** NH   **Length:** 3.9   **Opened:** 1876

When the Connecticut Central RR opened its main line between East Hartford and Springfield in 1876, it also completed this line as part of its Westway Branch. The line became part of the hapless New York & New England RR in 1880 and ultimately a component of the NH in 1898. In 1907 trolley wire was hung above its tracks, and electric cars provided passenger service until the late 1920s, when the wires came down.

244

Matfield, MA   West Bridgewater, MA

Abandoned: 1963   **Railroad:** NH   **Length:** 1.9   **Opened:** 1888

The West Bridgewater Branch of the Old Colony RR ran from Easton to Matfield. The NH took over the Old Colony in 1892. This was the last of 4 segments to be abandoned; the earliest was in 1938 (see line 137). Passenger service ended in 1925.

245

Stepney, CT   Botsford, CT

Abandoned: 1963   **Railroad:** NH   **Length:** 4.7   **Opened:** 1840

This segment once formed the Bridgeport-Pittsfield main line of the Housatonic RR. The Housatonic operated independently until 1892 when it was absorbed by the NH. Passenger service ceased in 1932 and remaining Bridgeport-Pittsfield trains were re-routed by way of Norwalk and Danbury.

246

Torrington, CT   Winsted, CT

Abandoned: 1963   **Railroad:** NH   **Length:** 7.9   **Opened:** 1849

This line formed part of the original main line of the Naugatuck RR. This railroad operated independently for many years until its absorption by the NH in 1887. Passenger service lasted until 1958.

247

Cumberland, RI   Plainville, MA

Abandoned: 1963   **Railroad:** NH   **Length:** 8   **Opened:** 1903

This line was built in 3 sections. The first, from Adamsdale Jct., MA, to Valley Falls, RI, opened in 1877 as part of the Franklin, MA-Valley Falls branch of the New York & New England RR (it was actually built by the Rhode Island & Massachusetts RR). The second, from Plainville to North Attleboro, was completed in 1890 by the Old Colony RR. In 1903 the NH, which now operated both lines, built the connecting track between North

Attleboro and Adamsdale Jct. Passenger service, which once included some Boston-Providence trains, ceased in 1938.

248

North Windham, CT   Pomfret, CT
Abandoned: 1963   **Railroad:** NH   **Length:** 14   **Opened:** 1872
The Boston, Hartford & Erie RR opened this segment in 1872 as part of its Boston-to-Providence/New Haven main line. It became a component of the New York & New England RR in 1875 and ultimately part of the NH in 1898. Daily Boston-Hartford passenger trains used the route until August 1955 when severe floods destroyed a bridge near Putnam and took the line out of service. Passenger service never resumed but freight trains returned for a few more years.

249

East Alburgh, VT   Rouses Point, NY
Abandoned: 1962   **Railroad:** CV   **Length:** 7.3   **Opened:** 1851
The Vermont & Canada RR constructed this line, but it was leased and operated by the Vermont Central RR as part of its main line to Canada. In 1873 the Vermont Central became the CV. This line featured a unique gauntlet bridge enabling both the Rutland and the CV to utilize the line without employing a switch. Passenger service ended around 1930.

251

Burlington, VT   Rouses Point, VT
Abandoned: 1963   **Railroad:** RUT   **Length:** 40   **Opened:** 1899
The Rutland RR built this line across the islands of Lake Champlain in 1899 to give it a direct line to Rouses Point and Canada independent of the CV. It was built as the Rutland-Canada RR but always operated as part of the Rutland. Passenger service ended in 1953. It was last operated in 1961, and was abandoned along with the entire Rutland RR. Today 7.7 miles of the old right-of-way in Burlington carry the Burlington Waterfront Bikeway.

254

Guilford Mill Yard, ME   Derby, ME
Abandoned: 1964   **Railroad:** BAR   **Length:** 22   **Opened:** 1884
The broad gauge Bangor & Piscataquis RR built the first portion of this line in 1869 between Derby and Dover, and extended the line past Guilford Mill Yard in 1884. The BAR bought the line in 1891. Passenger service lasted until 1958.

254A

Enfield, ME   Howland, ME
Abandoned: ca. 1963   **Railroad:** MC   **Length:** 3.5   **Opened:** 1907
In 1890 the MC opened a short branch line from Enfield to Montague, ME, and around 1907 extended it a short distance to Howland. It appears to have been operated only for freight.

255

Rising, MA   West Stockbridge, MA
Abandoned: 1964   **Railroad:** NH   **Length:** 6.7   **Opened:** 1843
This segment formed part of the State Line Branch of the Housatonic RR, which in fact had served as the original main line of that railroad for 7 years. The NH absorbed the Housatonic in 1892. Passenger service ended in 1928, but for many years the line carried through freight trains for interchange with the B&A at State Line.

256

Cranes (Taunton), MA   Mansfield, MA
Abandoned: 1965   **Railroad:** NH   **Length:** 8.5   **Opened:** 1836
The Taunton Branch RR opened this line in 1836, one of the earliest branch lines to be built in New England. This eventually became the New Bedford RR and in 1879 a part of the Old Colony RR. The NH took charge in 1893. For many years this formed part of a through route from New Bedford to Framingham and Fitchburg, but in 1955 a segment of 1750 feet in Mansfield was abandoned to eliminate a grade crossing. Passenger service ended at that time, but freight trains continued to serve this line from Taunton.

257

Canaan, CT [1570 ft W]   Lakeville (Salisbury), CT [1400 ft W]
Abandoned: 1965   **Railroad:** NH   **Length:** 9.5   **Opened:** 1871
Built by the Connecticut Western RR as part of its main line from Hartford to the Hudson River, this eventually became the Central New England RR in 1898. It passed to the NH in 1927, at which time passenger service was discontinued.

258

Colchester, CT   Amston, CT
Abandoned: 1965   **Railroad:** NH   **Length:** 4   **Opened:** 1877
This was the Colchester Branch of the Boston & New York Air-Line RR. It became part of the NH in 1882. Passenger service lasted until around 1927.

259

Plainville, MA   Wrentham, MA
Abandoned: ca. 1965   **Railroad:** NH   **Length:** 3   **Opened:** 1890
The Old Colony RR built this line as part of what it intended to be a new through route between Boston and Providence. The NH acquired the line 3 years later and continued to run passenger trains between Boston and Providence over the route until 1938, when all passenger service ceased.

260

Portland, CT   Columbia (Willimantic), CT
Abandoned: 1965   **Railroad:** NH   **Length:** 25   **Opened:** 1873
The New Haven, Middletown & Willimantic RR built this railroad as part of what they hoped would be a new direct New York-to-Boston line. The line soon failed and was reorganized in 1875 as the Boston & New York Air-Line RR, ever since known as the Air Line route. The NH leased the line in 1882. Between 1891 and 1895 the famous "White Train" used this line on its way from New York to Boston. The Boston-New York through trains lasted until 1924, and all passenger service was gone by 1937. Today 7 miles of the

line between East Hampton and Marlborough is a popular recreational trail, Airline South State Park Trail. The most prominent features are the Lyman and Rapallo Viaducts at East Hampton, former steel viaducts that were covered by earth fill during World War<N>I.

261

Providence, RI   Olneyville, RI
Abandoned: 1965   **Railroad:** NH   **Length:** 1.4   **Opened:** 1873
This short branch was the last remnant of the Providence & Springfield, which had built this line as part of its main line. The Providence & Springfield had hopes of opening a new route to the West from Providence, but the tracks never got beyond Douglas, MA. The New York & New England RR took over the line in 1890, and the NH assumed control in 1898. Passenger service ended around 1931.

262

River Point, RI   Arkright, RI
Abandoned: 1965   **Railroad:** NH   **Length:** 2.3   **Opened:** 1874
The Pawtuxet Valley RR built this line under the auspices of the Hartford, Providence & Fishkill RR, which operated the line upon completion. It later was expanded and transferred to the New York & New England RR, the New York, Providence & Boston, and finally, in 1892, to the NH. Passenger service ended around 1926.

263

South Dennis, MA   North Eastham, MA
Abandoned: 1965   **Railroad:** NH   **Length:** 18.6   **Opened:** 1871
The Cape Cod Central RR built this line as an extension of the Cape Cod RR. In 1873 the Old Colony RR took over and extended the rails to Provincetown. The line passed to the NH in 1893. Passenger service ended in 1938, although it was revived briefly in 1940.

264

West Roxbury, MA   Dedham, MA
Abandoned: 1965   **Railroad:** NH   **Length:** 2.3   **Opened:** 1850
The Boston & Providence RR built this line as an extension of its Dedham Branch (Readville-Dedham). First the Old Colony RR in 1888 and then the NH in 1893 operated the line, which proved so popular that a second track was added. In 1926 the NH began running commuter trains using this as a loop route that enabled trains to operate in and out of Boston without the need to turn around. The loop service ended in 1938 and remaining passenger trains were discontinued 2 years later. At that time the line was taken out of service, and it sat unused for another 25 years. Part of the line was said to be used to store locomotives awaiting scrapping.

265

Hartland, ME   Harmony, ME
Abandoned: 1966   **Railroad:** MC   **Length:** 9.2   **Opened:** 1899
Built by the Sabasticook & Moosehead Lake RR, this was an extension of that railroad's line from Pittsfield to Harmony. It became part of the MC in 1911. Passenger service was discontinued around 1939. The line had been out of service since 1963.

266

Atlantic, MA   Quincy, MA
Abandoned: 1966   **Railroad:** NH   **Length:** 4.7   **Opened:** 1845
This segment formed part of the original main line of the Old Colony RR from Boston to Plymouth. As the Old Colony system expanded, it carried ever-increasing numbers of commuter trains in and out of Boston. After the NH absorbed the Old Colony in 1893, traffic continued to grow; by 1913 the line had been increased to 4 tracks. In 1959, after many years of trying, the NH was permitted to abandon passenger service on the Old Colony lines. Freight service continued on this segment until 1966, when the MBTA took the right of way to construct its Red Line rapid transit extension to Quincy along this route (opened 1971). Recently, the MBTA and the state of Massachusetts have rebuilt the rail line alongside the transit line in order to restore passenger service on the Old Colony lines.

267

Marlboro Jct., MA   Marlboro, MA
Abandoned: 1966   **Railroad:** NH   **Length:** 1.5   **Opened:** 1855
The Marlboro Branch was built by the Agricultural Branch RR (from Framingham Centre), but operated by the Boston & Worcester RR until 1867. Around that time it was taken over by the Boston, Clinton & Fitchburg RR, which became part of the Old Colony RR in 1879. The NH absorbed the Old Colony system in 1893. Passenger service to Marlboro continued until 1958, and the line was abandoned 8 years later.

267A

at Norwich, CT
Abandoned: 1966   **Railroad:** NH   **Length:** 0.5   **Opened:** 1854
This short line connected the Norwich stations of the Norwich & Worcester RR (later NH) and the New London, Willimantic & Palmer RR (later CV). The Norwich & Worcester constructed the line so its trains would have direct access to New London. It became largely obsolete in 1899 when the NH, successor to the Norwich & Worcester, extended its Norwich-Allyns Point line to Groton, which gave it a direct rail connection to New London. Trackage rights over the CV were abandoned. The line appears to have been used for limited freight interchange for some time afterwards.

268

Whittenton Jct. (Taunton), MA   Raynham, MA   Easton, MA
Abandoned: 1966   **Railroad:** NH   **Length:** 9.7   **Opened:** 1882
This line was built as two separate segments. The tracks between Raynham and Easton were part of the main line of the Dighton & Somerset RR (completed 1866), which had become a part of the Old Colony & Newport RR. The Dighton & Somerset ran from Braintree (on the Old Colony) to Fall River. In 1882 the Old Colony decided to consolidate all passenger operations in Taunton at a station on its New Bedford & Taunton line (New Bedford-Mansfield). A new branch was constructed from Raynham (on the Dighton & Somerset) to a point on the New Bedford & Taunton (Whittenton Jct.), and nearly all trains were rerouted this way. The NH finally ended all passenger service on this segment in 1958. By 1966 there was not enough freight to justify retaining the line.

269

Farmington, CT   Collinsville, CT
Abandoned: 1968   **Railroad:** NH   **Length:** 7.9   **Opened:** 1850
The New Haven & Northampton RR had opened an 8-mile branch from Farmington, CT, to Collinsville, CT, in 1850, at the time its main line was constructed. In 1870 the line was extended another 5 miles to Pine Meadow, and 1876 another mile to New Hartford. The branch passed to the NH in 1887. Passenger service lasted until around 1928.

270

Millis, MA   West Medway, MA
Abandoned: 1967   **Railroad:** NH   **Length:** 3.7   **Opened:** 1862
The New York & Boston RR produced this segment as part of its main line between Brookline, Mass., and Woonsocket, RI. The section from Millis to Medway opened in 1861 and to West Medway the following year. Eventually the line passed to the New York & New England RR and in 1898, the NH. Passenger service on the line, which consisted of commuter trains to Boston, was suspended in 1938 but restored in 1940 and continued until 1966. Without passenger trains the line served no purpose and was abandoned.

271

Plainfield, CT   Coventry (Washington), RI
Abandoned: 1967   **Railroad:** NH   **Length:** 18.5   **Opened:** 1854
This line once formed part of the Hartford, Providence & Fishkill RR. By 1855 the tracks were completed 122 miles from Providence to Waterbury. The New York & New England RR absorbed the line in 1878, and 20 years later it passed to the NH. Passenger service ended around 1931. The portion of the right-of-way of this line in RI (8 miles) now carries the Trestle Trail.

271A

Loring Ave. (Salem), MA   Forest River (Salem), MA
Abandoned: ca. 1968   **Railroad:** B&M   **Length:** 0.5   **Opened:** 1839
This formed part of what later became 2 branch lines to Marblehead. It was built simultaneously with the original Eastern RR from Boston to Newburyport. It became the B&M's Marblehead Branch in 1884. Passenger trains continued until 1959.

272

Falmouth, MA   Woods Hole, MA
Abandoned: 1968   **Railroad:** NH   **Length:** 3.3   **Opened:** 1872
This formed the outermost part of the NH's Woods Hole Branch. The Cape Cod RR had built this line in order to relocate to Woods Hole the ferries that operated out of Hyannis for Marthas Vineyard and Nantucket. The Old Colony RR took over the Cape Cod RR about the time the branch was completed; in 1893 it passed to the NH. For many years trains brought passengers to and from the Woods Hole ferries. When passenger service ceased in 1964, the line was taken out of service. Today the right of way carries the popular bike path, the Falmouth Shining Sea Trail.

273

Haddam, CT   Laurel (Middletown), CT
Abandoned: 1968   **Railroad:** NH   **Length:** 5.5   **Opened:** 1871
The Connecticut Valley RR completed its line from Hartford to Old Saybrook in 1871. The NH took over the line in 1887. Passenger service ended around 1931. In 1968 the NH abandoned the line between Laurel and Old Saybrook (22.3 miles), but 3 years later the Valley RR restored service to the tracks between Essex and Deep River for steam passenger excursion trains. By 1980 it was operating between Old Saybrook and Chester, and today Valley RR trains go as far north as Haddam, leaving only the last 5.5 miles abandoned.

274

Simsbury, CT   West Simsbury, CT
Abandoned: 1968   **Railroad:** NH   **Length:** 0.9   **Opened:** 1871
Built by the Connecticut Western RR as part of its main line from Hartford to the Hudson River, this segment became the Central New England RR in 1898. It became part of the New Haven in 1927, at which time passenger service was discontinued. Today the Stratton Brook Trail follows its right-of-way.

275

South Barre, MA   Waterville, MA
Abandoned: 1968   **Railroad:** PC   **Length:** 22   **Opened:** 1873
Shortly before the Ware River RR completed its line between Palmer and Winchenden in 1873, it was leased by the B&A. Passenger service ended in 1948. When the B&A secured this abandonment in 1968, the final two miles of the line between Waterville and Winchendon were transferred to the B&M.

277

Florence, MA   Easthampton, MA
Abandoned: 1969   **Railroad:** PC   **Length:** 7.4   **Opened:** 1868
The New Haven & Northampton RR built this line as part of its Williamsburg Branch, which connected to its main line in Northampton. The NH took control of the line in 1887 and ended passenger service around 1922. When the final customer, a fuel oil dealer, converted to trucks in June 1968, the line was no longer used.

278

Franklin Jct., MA   Klondike (Putnam), CT
Abandoned: 1969   **Railroad:** PC   **Length:** 31.9   **Opened:** 1854
The Norfolk Central RR opened its line from Dedham to Blackstone in 1849. Four years later the Boston & New York Central RR took over the line and extended it to Mechanicsville (Putnam). In 1867 the Boston, Hartford & Erie acquired the line, and 8 years later it became part of the New York & New England system. After the line was extended to Willimantic in 1872 it became part of a through route from Boston to New York and Hartford. Once it became part of the NH in 1898, however, the line declined as a through route. Boston-New York service ended in 1924, but trains ran to Hartford until 1955, when floods brought an abrupt end to passenger service west of Blackstone. Commuter service between Blackstone and Boston lasted until 1966 when Franklin became the terminus of MBTA rail service. For many years the line was used for occasional

wide loads that could not clear other routes. These through movements ended in March 1968 when floods destroyed a bridge at Blackstone, and the NH (later PC) did not feel that the traffic justified its rebuilding.

279

at Meriden, CT
Abandoned: 1969   **Railroad:** PC   **Length:** 1.5   **Opened:** 1885
This line once constituted part of the Meriden & Cromwell and later the Meriden, Waterbury & Conncecticut River. The line was out of service 1896-98, before the NH restored service. In 1906 the NH electrified the line, and electric cars operated between Meriden and Middletown until 1932. After the abandonment of part of the line between Meriden and Westfield in 1938 this became the York Hill Quarry Track. It was last used in 1966.

280

at East Somerville, MA
Abandoned: 1969   **Railroad:** PC   **Length:** 0.7   **Opened:** 1852
This segment was part of the Grand Junction RR, a freight-only belt line that originally connected the docks of East Boston with Somerville. The line was out of service between 1857 and 1869, when it became part of the B&A. When the PC, which had taken over the B&A in 1968, abandoned this line, it obtained trackage rights over parallel B&M yard trackage.

280A

Salem, MA   Salem Harbor (Phillips Wharf), MA
Abandoned: ca. 1970   **Railroad:** B&M   **Length:** 1   **Opened:** 1850
When the Salem & Lowell RR (operated by the Lowell & Lawrence RR) opened its line to Salem in 1850, it built this freight-only branch to the docks in Salem. (The Salem & Lowell reached Salem via trackage rights over the Essex RR). The Boston & Lowell took over the line in 1858, and later attempted to make Salem a major coal port utilizing this branch. For many years trains loaded coal from the wharves and carried it to Lowell and beyond. After the B&M acquired the line in 1887 it declined to a minor local branch.

281

at Bridgeport, CT
Abandoned: 1970   **Railroad:** PC   **Length:** 0.7   **Opened:** 1840
This segment once formed part of the Bridgeport-Pittsfield main line of the Housatonic RR. The Housatonic operated independently until 1892 when it was absorbed by the NH. Passenger service ceased in 1932 and remaining Bridgeport-Pittsfield trains were re-routed by way of Norwalk and Danbury. After the abandonment of the section between Bridgeport and Stepney in 1938 the NH retained the first mile or so of this line in Bridgeport for local freight. This section was abandoned in 1970 so the state could relocate Route 25.

282

East Providence, RI   Providence, RI
Abandoned: 1971   **Railroad:** PC   **Length:** 0.7   **Opened:** 1835
This line formed part of the original main line of the Boston & Providence RR. In 1847 that railroad opened a more direct line into the city, leaving this line at the end of what

became the East Providence branch. The city of Providence is said to have wanted this land for a park. The bridge was out of service before the abandonment.

283

Manchester, CT   Columbia, CT
Abandoned: 1970   **Railroad:** PC   **Length:** 19.4   **Opened:** 1863
This section was completed in 1849 by the Hartford, Providence and Fishkill RR as part of its main line between Providence and Waterbury. This railroad subsequently became part of the New York & New England RR in 1878 and 20 years later a branch of the NH. In addition to through steam-powered trains, the line between Manchester and Vernon was electrified in 1907 and electric cars operated until the 1920s. Passenger trains between Boston and Hartford plied this route until August 1955 when floods closed the line and passenger service was suspended, never to resume. Local freight kept the line in business for another 15 years, but ultimately was not enough to justify continued operation. The tracks in Manchester and Vernon remain in place. Between Vernon and Columbia the right of way is used by the Hop River State Park Trail.

284

Vernon, CT   Rockville, CT
Abandoned: 1970   **Railroad:** PC   **Length:** 4.4   **Opened:** 1863
This branch was chartered and built as the Rockville RR, but was operated by the Hartford, Providence & Fishkill RR, with which it connected at Vernon. It subsequently became a branch of the New York & New England RR (1878) and the NH (1898). In 1907 it was electrified and trolleys operated over the line until the 1920s. Passenger service on the Rockville Branch ended around 1929.

285

North Station (Boston), MA   South Station (Boston), MA
Abandoned: 1970   **Railroad:** UF   **Length:** 1.7   **Opened:** 1872
This diminutive short line operated mostly on Boston city streets between North and South Stations. It was always operated solely for freight, and most operations took place at night. After the merger of the B&A and the NH into the PC in 1969, it was largely closed as an interchange route. Part of the line was taken out of service in 1969 and abandonment followed less than a year later.

286

at Newburyport, MA
Abandoned: 1971   **Railroad:** B&M   **Length:** 1.9   **Opened:** 1872
The Newburyport City RR opened this freight-only line in 1872 to connect the wharves of Newburyport with the Eastern RR main line. A connection was also built with the B&M's Newburyport line. It became part of the B&M in 1884, and was in use as a freight branch for nearly a century.

287

Hoosac Tunnel, MA   Readsboro, VT
Abandoned: 1971   **Railroad:** HTW   **Length:** 10.9   **Opened:** 1885
The Deerfield River Co. opened a 3-foot gauge logging railroad from Hoosac Tunnel to Readsboro in 1885. The following year it transferred the railroad to the newly-formed Hoosac Tunnel & Wilmington RR (which operated it as a common carrier). An extension

to Wilmington, VT, opened in 1891. In 1913 the line was converted to standard gauge. Regular passenger service ended in 1927. The extension north of Wilmington was abandoned in 1938 (see line 125). The line continued as an independently-operated freight short line until 1971, when it was abandoned rather than face a costly relocation necessitated by the construction of the Bear Swamp hydroelectric project.

288

Hinckley, ME   Skowhegan, ME
Abandoned: 1971   **Railroad:** MC   **Length:** 4.8   **Opened:** 1857
The standard gauge Somerset & Kennebec RR built this as part of its line from Augusta to Skowhegan. Reorganized as the Portland & Kennebec RR in 1864, it became a part of the MC in 1870. Passenger trains last ran around 1946.

289

Weir Village (Taunton), MA   Dighton, MA
Abandoned: 1971   **Railroad:** PC   **Length:** 3   **Opened:** 1866
The Old Colony & Newport RR built this segment as part of its Dighton & Somerset main line between Boston and Fall River. The Old Colony system became part of the NH in 1893. Passenger and freight trains used the line daily until 1932 when the NH abandoned a drawbridge across the Taunton River. This brought an end to passenger and through freight service.

290

Jaffrey, NH   Peterboro, NH
Abandoned: 1972   **Railroad:** B&M   **Length:** 5.5   **Opened:** 1871
The Monadnock RR opened this line in 1871, part of its route between Winchendon, MA, and Peterborough, NH. The Boston, Barre & Gardner RR operated the line between 1874 and 1880 and then it became a branch of the Cheshire RR. The Fitchburg took over 10 years later, and in 1900, the B&M. At one time it formed part of a through route between Worcester and Concord, NH. Passenger service ended in 1953.

291

Keene, NH   Cold River, NH
Abandoned: 1972   **Railroad:** B&M   **Length:** 20.7   **Opened:** 1849
This line formed part of the Cheshire RR, which stretched from South Ashburnham, MA, to Bellows Falls, VT. The entire line was completed in 1849. The Cheshire acquired other small railroads and operated independently until 1890 when it became part of the Fitchburg RR system. In 1900 the B&M absorbed the Fitchburg. In the first half of the twentieth century this was a major passenger route between Boston and Montreal via Fitchburg, Bellows Falls, and Rutland. When the Rutland RR ended all passenger service on its Vermont lines in 1953, the line was deprived of most of its passenger traffic, and passenger service ended in 1958. The subsequent collapse of the Rutland RR in the early 1960s further reduced freight traffic and set the stage for its abandonment in the 1970s.

292

Mt. Whittier, NH   Conway, NH
Abandoned: 1972   **Railroad:** B&M   **Length:** 11.8   **Opened:** 1872
The Eastern RR constructed this line as an extension of the Portsmouth, Great Falls & Conway RR, which it leased. The B&M took over the line in 1884. Passenger service lasted

until 1961. In 1972 the B&M abandoned the entire line from Intervale to Mt. Whittier, but the following year the Conway Scenic RR reopened 5 miles of the line between Conway and North Conway and has continued to operate this segment ever since.

293

Newton Jct., NH   Merrimac, MA
Abandoned: 1972   **Railroad:** B&M   **Length:** 4.4   **Opened:** 1873
The West Amesbury Branch RR was built to connect that Massachusetts town with the B&M main line (across the state line in New Hampshire). The B&M leased the line on completion and operated it afterwards as a B&M branch. Even though West Amesbury was renamed Merrimac in 1876, the line continued to be called the West Amesbury Branch for many years. Passenger service ended in 1927. The line was last used in August 1971.

294

Winchendon, MA   Swanzey, NH
Abandoned: 1972   **Railroad:** B&M   **Length:** 20.6   **Opened:** 1849
This line formed part of the Cheshire RR, which stretched from South Ashburnham, MA, to Bellows Falls, VT. The entire line was completed in 1849. The Cheshire acquired other small railroads and operated independently until 1890 when it became part of the Fitchburg RR system. In 1900 the B&M absorbed the Fitchburg. In the first half of the twentieth century this was a major passenger route between Boston and Montreal via Fitchburg, Bellows Falls, and Rutland. When the Rutland RR ended all passenger service on its Vermont lines in 1953, the line was deprived of most of its passenger traffic, and passenger service ended in 1958. The subsequent collapse of the Rutland RR in the early 1960s further reduced freight traffic and set the stage for its abandonment in the 1970s.

296

Cromwell, CT   Rocky Hill, CT
Abandoned: ca. 1972   **Railroad:** NH   **Length:** 3.9   **Opened:** 1872
The Connecticut Valley RR was responsible for this segment, which formed part of its main line between Hartford and Old Saybrook. The NH took over the line in 1887. Passenger service was discontinued in 1933. The line was last used in January 1970.

297

Metcalfs, MA   Milford, MA
Abandoned: 1972   **Railroad:** PC   **Length:** 4.6   **Opened:** 1848
This formed part of the Boston & Worcester RR's Milford Branch (Framingham-Milford). The Boston & Worcester became the B&A in 1867. Passenger service ended in 1959.

298

North Brookfield, MA   East Brookfield, MA
Abandoned: 1972   **Railroad:** PC   **Length:** 4.2   **Opened:** 1876
Built as the North Brookfield RR, it was leased by the B&A on completion and always operated as a B&A branch. Passenger service ceased in 1935. The line was taken out of service in 1970.

299

South Norwalk, CT   Wilsons Point, CT [end of track]
Abandoned: 1973   **Railroad:** PC   **Length:** 0.8   **Opened:** 1884
This was the last remnant of the Wilsons Point Branch. The line was constructed by the Danbury & Norwalk RR to reach Wilsons Point, reputed to have one of the finest harbors on Long Island Sound. This segment formed part of a new Boston-New York passenger line, utilizing the NY&NE, the Danbury & Norwalk, and steamships from Wilsons Point to New York City. Barges transported freight cars to New York, Long Island, even New Jersey. This operation came to an abrupt halt in 1892 when the rival NH purchased the Danbury & Norwalk. By 1894 passenger service on the branch was gone, and the line was relegated to a minor branch line. The outer 0.6 miles of the branch was abandoned in 1938 (line 121).

300

South Spencer, MA   Spencer, MA
Abandoned: 1972   **Railroad:** PC   **Length:** 2.2   **Opened:** 1879
The Spencer RR built this short line to connect Spencer with the main line of the B&A. On completion the B&A leased the line and ever afterwards operated it as a B&A branch line. Passenger service ended around 1932.

301

Bristol, RI   Warren, RI
Abandoned: 1973   **Railroad:** PC   **Length:** 4   **Opened:** 1855
The Providence, Warren & Bristol RR built its original line into Bristol from Providence. This railroad continued to operate the line until 1891 when the Old Colony RR and later the NH took over. The line was electrified between 1900 and 1934. Passenger service with gas electric cars continued until 1937. Today the right-of-way is used by the East Bay Bicycle Path.

302

Highland Jct. (Waterbury), CT   Watertown, CT
Abandoned: 1973   **Railroad:** PC   **Length:** 4.9   **Opened:** 1870
The Naugatuck RR built this branch to Watertown in 1870. The NH gained the line in 1887. Around 1925 passenger service was discontinued.

303

Washington St. (West Quincy), MA   Printing Plant (West Quincy), MA
Abandoned: 1973   **Railroad:** PC   **Length:** 0.8   **Opened:** 1873
The Old Colony RR constructed this segment, part of a branch which ran from Atlantic to Braintree. It became a NH branch in 1893. Passenger service ended in 1940.

304

Keene, NH   Swanzey,NH
Abandoned: 1975   **Railroad:** B&M   **Length:** 1.1   **Opened:** 1848
This short segment once formed part of the Cheshire RR, which stretched from South Ashburnham, MA, to Bellows Falls, VT. The entire line was completed in 1849. The Cheshire acquired other small railroads and operated independently until 1890 when it became part of the Fitchburg RR system. In 1900 the B&M absorbed the Fitchburg. In the

first half of the twentieth century this was a major passenger route between Boston and Montreal via Fitchburg, Bellows Falls, and Rutland. When the Rutland RR ended all passenger service on its Vermont lines in 1953, the line was deprived of most of its passenger traffic, and passenger service ended in 1958. In 1981 the B&M applied to abandon this segment, claiming the rails had been taken up by mistake in 1975!

304A

Monticello, ME   Bridgewater, ME
Abandoned: 1975   **Railroad:** BAR   **Length:** 10.1   **Opened:** 1895
This was part of the original main line of the BAR. Passenger service ended in 1961. Freight traffic had begun to decline seriously after 1953, and by 1971 only 125 carloads were loaded or unloaded during the year.

305

Waterville, MA   Winchendon, MA
Abandoned: 1984   **Railroad:** B&M   **Length:** 2   **Opened:** 1873
This short segment was a remnant of the Ware River RR. Shortly before the Ware River completed its line between Palmer and Winchenden in 1873 it was leased by the B&A. Passenger service ended in 1948. When the B&A (PC) abandoned the line between Waterville and South Barre in 1968 it left this segment isolated. It was transferred to the B&M, who operated the line until it was abandoned.

307

Quebec Jct., NH   Waumbek Jct., NH
Abandoned: 1977   **Railroad:** MC   **Length:** 2.5   **Opened:** 1889
The MC built this as part of its Upper Coos RR. Passenger service ended around 1933.

307A

East Bridgewater, MA   Westdale, MA
Abandoned: 1976   **Railroad:** PC   **Length:** 1.9   **Opened:** 1885
This abandonment constituted two lines that were built separately but had long been operated together. The section between East Bridgewater and Elmwood was once part of the Bridgewater Branch of the Old Colony RR. Built in 1847, it originally connected Whitman and Stanley. In 1885 the Old Colony built a short connection between Elmwood and Westdale, on the Old Colony's Fall River line. The NH began operating the lines in 1893. Passenger service lasted until 1925. After the NH abandoned most of the Bridge-water Branch in 1937 (see lines 109 and 120), it left only the track between East Bridgewater and Westdale in service.

308

Hazardville, CT   East Windsor, CT
Abandoned: 1976   **Railroad:** PC   **Length:** 6   **Opened:** 1876
This line was part of the Connecticut Central RR, which opened its line between Hartford and Springfield in 1876. At first the line was operated by the Connecticut Valley RR under lease (as a logical extension of its Old Saybrook-Hartford main line), but soon it was canceled, leaving the Connecticut Central to operate on its own until 1880 when it was leased to the New York & New England RR. The NH took over in 1898. Passenger service ended around 1933. The line was taken out of service in 1972 and the PC put it up for

abandonment. When Conrail took over the PC system in 1976 this line was not included and so abandoned.

308A

at Meriden, CT
Abandoned: 1976   **Railroad:** PC   **Length:** 2.9   **Opened:** 1888

This line once constituted part of the Meriden & Cromwell and later the Meriden, Waterbury & Conncecticut River. The line was out of service 1896-98, before the NH restored service. In 1906 the NH electrified the line, and electric cars operated between Meriden and Middletown until 1932. After 1969 it was virtually the only remaining part of the old Meriden, Waterbury & Connecticut River. This trackage was connecting track east and west of Meriden station (Quarry Jct.). which linked it to the New Haven-Hartford main line.

310

Millbury Jct., MA   Millbury, MA
Abandoned: 1976   **Railroad:** PC   **Length:** 3   **Opened:** 1837

The Boston & Worcester built this short line as one of its earliest branches. It subsequently became part of the B&A (1867) and the PC (1968). Passenger service ended in 1941. When Conrail took over operations of old PC lines, it did not take this one. The rails were removed in 1980 after the right-of-way had been sold to three private parties.

311

Stoughton, MA   Easton, MA
Abandoned: 1976   **Railroad:** PC   **Length:** 5.6   **Opened:** 1866

The portion of this line between Stoughton and North Easton was built in 1855 as the Easton Branch RR, which was leased to the Boston & Providence RR. In 1866 the Dighton & Somerset RR, a subsidiary of the Old Colony & Newport RR, opened its main line between Braintree and Fall River. At this time the Easton Branch RR was acquired from the Boston & Providence and the section between Stoughton Jct. and North Easton was incorporated into its line. The initial part of the branch from Stoughton to Stoughton Jct. at first became a freight-only branch, but later became part of a new Boston-Fall River route. The section from North Easton to Easton was part of the new Dighton & Somerset main line. Passenger service ended in 1958, and the line was abandoned rather than being included in the new Conrail system.

312

Westfield, MA   Simsbury, CT
Abandoned: 1976   **Railroad:** PC   **Length:** 17   **Opened:** 1856

The New Haven & Northampton began construction of this part of its main line in 1846 and opened the section between Simsbury and Granby, CT, in 1850. In 1856 the line was extended through Westfield to Northampton, MA. Until 1869 the line was operated under lease to the New York & New Haven RR, then independently until 1887 when it was absorbed into the growing NH system. Passenger service ended around 1928. The PC sought to abandon this segment as early as 1971, but actual abandonment did not occur until 5 years later. Today, the Farmington Valley Greenway, a biking trail, utilizes 2 miles of the old right of way in Simsbury.

313

Wrentham, MA   East Walpole, MA
Abandoned: 1976   **Railroad:** PC   **Length:** 13.4   **Opened:** 1892
The Old Colony RR opened the section between Cedar and Wrentham in 1890 and the rest of this segment in 1892. The railroad intended this line to be part of another through line between Boston and Providence. The NH acquired the line a year later and continued to run passenger trains between Boston and Providence over the route until 1938, when all passenger service ceased.

313A

East Providence, RI   Warren, RI
Abandoned: ca. 1981   **Railroad:** P&W   **Length:** 9.6   **Opened:** 1855
The Providence, Warren & Bristol RR originally built this line. At first the Boston & Providence RR operated the railroad, but after 1860 the line operated on its own. This continued until 1891 when the Old Colony RR took over the line, and 2 years later, in turn, gave way to the NH. In 1900 the NH electrified the line, and ran electric cars between Providence and Bristol and Fall River over the tracks. Electric operation ended in 1934, but passenger service continued until 1937. When the PC exited the railroad business in 1976 the line was transferred to the Providence & Worcester. The tracks have been removed and the right-of-way converted to the East Bay Bicycle Path.

313B

Lowell (City Line), MA   Chelmsford Centre, MA
Abandoned: 1976   **Railroad:** PC   **Length:** 2   **Opened:** 1871
This segment once formed part of the main line of the Framingham & Lowell RR. In 1879 it became part of the Old Colony RR system and in 1893 a branch of the New Haven. Passenger service ceased in 1933, but throughout the NH period it was used for through freight trains out of northern New England via the B&M at Lowell. These became less frequent once the PC took over the NH in 1969. In 1976, this segment was not included in the former PC lines taken over by Conrail, and so was abandoned. Some of the track remains in place.

313C

Riverside, MA   Newton Lower Falls, MA
Abandoned: 1976   **Railroad:** PC   **Length:** 1.4   **Opened:** 1847
The Boston & Worcester RR constructed this short branch. It became part of the B&A in 1867. Between 1904 and 1930 it was electrified and used by trolleys. Conventional passenger service ended in 1957. After 1972 only the first mile between Riverside station and the MBTA's Riverside trolley yards remained in service.

314

Carson Siding, ME   Sweden Siding, ME
Abandoned: 1978   **Railroad:** AV   **Length:** 7.2   **Opened:** 1912
This line was built around 1912 by the AV, an electric railroad. It converted to diesel operation in 1946 and discontinued passenger operations at the same time.

315

South Lagrange, ME   Packard, ME
Abandoned: 1977   **Railroad:** BAR   **Length:** 28   **Opened:** 1907
Passenger service on this line ended around 1930.

316

Claremont, NH (Washington St.)   Newport, NH
Abandoned: 1977   **Railroad:** C&C   **Length:** 11   **Opened:** 1872
The Sugar River RR built this line as an extension of the Concord & Claremont RR. It became part of the C&C in 1873, but passed to the B&M in 1887. In 1954 the B&M sold the line to a new Claremont & Concord RR. Passenger service ended the year following. Today 8 miles of the right of way forms the Sugar River Recreation Trail.

317

Hollister, VT   Proctor, VT   Center Rutland, VT
Abandoned: 1977   **Railroad:** C&P   **Length:** 9.2   **Opened:** 1903
Although a common carrier, the C&P was basically a quarry railroad. The line from Florence Jct. to West Rutland was completed in 1888, and the line was extended to Hollister around 1903.

317A

Quincy, MA   Braintree, MA
Abandoned: 1978   **Railroad:** CR   **Length:** 2.1   **Opened:** 1845
This segment formed part of the original main line of the Old Colony RR from Boston to Plymouth. As the Old Colony system expanded it carried ever-increasing numbers of commuter trains in and out of Boston. After the NH absorbed the Old Colony in 1893 traffic continued to grow; by 1913 the line had been increased to 4 tracks. In 1959, after many years of trying, the NH was permitted to abandon passenger service on the Old Colony lines. Freight service continued on this segment until 1966, when the MBTA took the right of way to construct its Red Line rapid transit extension to Quincy along this route (opened 1971). After the transit line opened a track was provided for freight service between Quincy and Braintree, but this was abandoned in 1978. The state is currently restoring rail commuter service to the South Shore and this line should be back in service (for passengers) in the near future.

317B

Center Rutland, VT   West Rutland, VT
Abandoned: ca. 1977   **Railroad:** C&P   **Length:** 2   **Opened:** 1888
Although a common carrier, the C&P was basically a quarry line. This route was opened in conjunction with the line between Florence Jct. and West Rutland.

318

Ayer Jct., ME   Eastport, ME
Abandoned: 1978   **Railroad:** MC   **Length:** 16.6   **Opened:** 1898
This branch was built at the same time as the Washington County RR, of which it formed a part. The MC began operating the line in 1904 and absorbed it in 1911. Passenger service ended in 1957. The tracks were taken up in 1980.

319

Caribou, ME   Stockholm, ME
Abandoned: 1979   **Railroad:** BAR   **Length:** 13.7   **Opened:** 1899
Passenger service was discontinued on this line in 1960.

320

South Acton, MA   Maynard, MA
Abandoned: 1979   **Railroad:** B&M   **Length:** 2.7   **Opened:** 1850
The Fitchburg RR used the charter of the Lancaster & Sterling to open a branch to Feltonville (Hudson), by way of Maynard, in 1850. In 1855 the branch was extended to Marlboro. This became part of the B&M in 1900. Passenger service ended in 1958, and afterwards the line was seldom used, except for a small part of the line at South Acton that served as a layover point for B&M commuter trains. By the time of abandonment the line beyond South Acton had been out of service for many years.

321

Bennington, NH   Hillsboro, NH
Abandoned: 1979   **Railroad:** B&M   **Length:** 8.4   **Opened:** 1878
This line was built by the Peterboro & Hillsboro RR. It became a B&M branch in 1889. Passenger service was discontinued around 1936.

322

Townsend, MA [0.7 mi W]   Greenville, NH
Abandoned: 1979   **Railroad:** B&M   **Length:** 12.9   **Opened:** 1850
The Peterborough and Shirley RR opened its line from Ayer to West Townsend, MA, in 1848 and reached its terminus at Greenville, NH, in 1850. Even before it was open the Peterborough & Shirley was leased by the Fitchburg RR, and after 1900 was a branch of the B&M. Passenger service ended in 1933, about the same time that the closing of Greenville's textile mills deprived the line of much of its traffic. It some how hung on until 1972, when floods took most of this segment out of operation. The most prominent feature of this line was an impressive steel trestle across the Souhegan River in Greenville; today, only the tall stone piers remain.

323

West Cambridge, MA   Bedford, MA
Abandoned: 1991   **Railroad:** B&M   **Length:** 11   **Opened:** 1873
The Lexington & Arlington RR completed a line from West Cambridge (on the Fitchburg RR) to Lexington in 1846. The Fitchburg leased the line until 1858, when it began operating independently. The Boston & Lowell RR acquired the line in 1870 and in 1873 extended the line (under the name of the Middlesex Central RR) through Bedford to Concord. The B&M took over operation of the line in 1887. Commuter rail service on the line declined after World War II, and by 1958 had been reduced to a single round trip. Subsidies kept the trains running until a blizzard in January 1977 shut down passenger operations. They never resumed. In 1979 the B&M received permission to abandon the line, but actually continued freight operation until 1981. The line was formally abandoned in 1991, to facilitate its conversion into a bike trail.

324

West Somerville, MA   North Cambridge, MA
Abandoned: 1979   **Railroad:** B&M   **Length:** 1.3   **Opened:** 1870
The Boston & Lowell RR constructed this line after it purchased control of the Lexington & Arlington RR in 1870. It thus connected that railroad with the Boston & Lowell main line in Somerville. In 1887 it became part of the B&M. In 1926 passenger trains from the Lexington & Arlington Branch were rerouted over the Fitchburg line and this became part of the B&M's freight cutoff. Most westbound freight trains used this line until 1979, when the B&M abandoned the line so that part of the right of way could be used by the MBTA to extend its Red Line transit to Alewife Brook station.

324A

West Hingham, MA   Nantasket Jct., MA
Abandoned: 1979   **Railroad:** CR   **Length:** 2   **Opened:** 1849
The South Shore RR opened this line in 1849. For a few years the Old Colony RR operated it, but for more than 20 years the line ran independently. The Old Colony took over the line in 1877, and was absorbed by the NH in 1893. Between 1896 and 1906 the line was electrified using a third rail. Passenger service continued over this line until the discontinuation of all Old Colony commuter routes in 1959. The line carried little freight and was abandoned. Today the MBTA and the state are seeking to rebuild the line to reintroduce rail commuter service to Greenbush.

325

North Anson, ME   Bingham, ME
Abandoned: 1979   **Railroad:** MC   **Length:** 16   **Opened:** 1890
The Somerset RY built this line as an extension of its original main line between Oakland and North Anson (1877). It was opened between North Anson and Solon in 1884 and completed to Bingham in 1890. It became part of the MC in 1907. Passenger service ended around 1933.

326

Houlton, ME   Monticello, ME
Abandoned: 1980   **Railroad:** BAR   **Length:** 10.1   **Opened:** 1895
This was part of the original main line of the BAR. Passenger service lasted until 1960.

327

Canal Jct. (Belchertown), MA   Bondsville (Palmer), MA
Abandoned: 1980   **Railroad:** B&M   **Length:** 6.8   **Opened:** 1887
This was constructed between 1878 and 1887 as part of the Boston- to-Northampton main line of the Massachusetts Central (later Central Massachusetts) RR. It was operated briefly by the Boston & Lowell RR before becoming part of the B&M in 1887. Passenger service ended in 1932.

328

Creamery, MA   Wheelwright, MA
Abandoned: 1980   **Railroad:** B&M   **Length:** 2.8   **Opened:** 1887
This also was constructed between 1878 and 1887 as part of the Boston-to-Northampton main line of the Massachusetts Central (later Central Massachusetts) RR. It was operated

briefly by the Boston & Lowell RR before becoming part of the B&M in 1887. Passenger service ended in 1932

329

Hudson, MA   Marlboro, MA
Abandoned: 1980   **Railroad:** B&M   **Length:** 4.7   **Opened:** 1855
The Fitchburg RR built this line as an extension of its existing branch from South Acton to Hudson. It became a B&M branch in 1900. Passenger service was discontinued in 1939.

329A

at Nashua, NH
Abandoned: ca. 1980   **Railroad:** B&M   **Length:** 2   **Opened:** 1873
This segment constituted the initial 2 miles of the Nashua, Acton & Boston RR, which once ran from Nashua to West Concord, MA. In 1876 the NA&B became part of New Hampshire's Concord RR system and in 1889 the Concord & Montreal, before passing to the B&M in 1895. Passenger service ended in 1924, and the following year the entire line except this segment was abandoned (see line 42). This track served some local industrial shippers until the 1970s.

330

Northampton, MA   Norwottuck, MA
Abandoned: 1980   **Railroad:** B&M   **Length:** 9.6   **Opened:** 1887
This was constructed between 1878 and 1887 as part of the Boston- to-Northampton main line of the Massachusetts Central (later Central Massachusetts) RR. It was operated for a few years by the Boston & Lowell RR before becoming part of the B&M in 1887. Passenger service ended in 1932. This right of way, including the bridge over the Connecticut River, now carries the Five College Bikeway.

331

Waltham North, MA   Berlin, MA
Abandoned: 1980   **Railroad:** B&M   **Length:** 21.7   **Opened:** 1881
This segment once formed part of the Boston-Northampton main line of the Massachusetts Central (Central Massachusetts) RR. The Boston & Lowell RR eventually took over operation of the line in 1886, and in turn passed it to the B&M in 1887. Passenger service out of Boston was provided on the entire segment until 1958, when Hudson became the terminus. After 1965 the trains went no farther than South Sudbury. Passenger service ended altogether in 1971, and local freight traffic was not enough to sustain the line.

331A

North Plymouth, MA   Plymouth, MA
Abandoned: ca. 1980   **Railroad:** CR   **Length:** 2   **Opened:** 1845
This line was built in 1845 as the final 2 miles of the Old Colony RR from Boston. After many years of independent operation it became a part of the NH in 1893. Passenger service ended in 1959, with the demise of Old Colony commuter lines. At the time of abandonment the line was out of service.

332

at Ware, MA
Abandoned: 1980   **Railroad:** B&M   **Length:** 1.4   **Opened:** 1887
This was constructed as part of the Boston-to-Northampton main line of the Massachusetts Central (later Central Massachusetts) RR. It was operated for a few years by the Boston & Lowell RR before becoming part of the B&M in 1887. Passenger service ended in 1932.

332A

Dedham, MA   East Dedham, MA
Abandoned: ca. 1980   **Railroad:** CR   **Length:** 0.9   **Opened:** 1834
This short segment once formed part of the Dedham branch. Constructed by the Boston & Providence RR at the time the latter was being built, it was the first branch line in New England. The Old Colony RR finally took over the Boston & Providence in 1888, and in 1893 the NH absorbed the Old Colony. Passenger service survived until 1967.

332B

Fitchville Jct. (Gibbs), CT   Fitchville, CT
Abandoned: ca. 1980   **Railroad:** CV   **Length:** 2   **Opened:** 1880
The CV built this freight-only branch to serve local industrial customers.

332C

Castleton, VT   Salem, NY
Abandoned: ca. 1980   **Railroad:** D&H   **Length:** 35   **Opened:** 1852
The Rutland & Washington RR was responsible for building this line. In 1865 it became part of the Rensselaer & Saratoga RR, and in 1871 it was absorbed by the D&H. Passenger trains last used the line around 1933. The VT portions of the old right-of-way have been converted into the Delaware & Hudson Recreation Trail.

333

Danvers, MA   Topsfield, MA
Abandoned: 1981   **Railroad:** B&M   **Length:** 5.2   **Opened:** 1854
The Danvers & Georgetown built this line as an extension of the Newburyport RR, which operated the line when it was completed. The B&M assumed control in 1860. Passenger service was provided until 1950. The line was taken out of service in 1977, and by the time of abandonment the right of way was overgrown with bushes, some of the rails had been removed, and the grade crossings were paved over.

334

East Manchester, NH   Rockingham Jct., NH
Abandoned: 1982   **Railroad:** B&M   **Length:** 27.2   **Opened:** 1861
In 1852 the Concord & Portsmouth RR opened its main line between its namesake cities. The portion of this segment between Rockingham Jct. and Candia formed part of this line. In 1858 the Concord RR leased the line. When the lease came up for renewal in 1861 the Concord demanded that the C&P abandon its main line between Candia and Concord and instead construct a connection between Candia and Manchester. The C&P would thus have to interchange all of its west end freight with the Concord RR, since the Concord monopolized rail service to Manchester (but not to the city of Concord). The line became

part of the Concord & Montreal RR in 1889 and the B&M in 1895. Passenger service was provided until 1954.

335

Epping, NH   Fremont, NH
Abandoned: 1982   **Railroad:** B&M   **Length:** 3.5   **Opened:** 1874
The Nashua & Rochester RR built this line as an extension of the Worcester & Nashua RR. After the B&M acquired it in 1886 it formed part of its Worcester, Nashua & Rochester division, a through route between Worcester and Rochester. Passenger service on the line ended in 1934.

335A

Machine Shop, MA   North Andover, MA
Abandoned: 1981   **Railroad:** B&M   **Length:** 0.5   **Opened:** 1848
This was a short remnant of the main line of the Essex RR between Salem and Lawrence, operated first by the Eastern RR and after 1884 by the B&M. Passenger service was discontinued in 1926, when most of the old Essex RR was abandoned.

336

Manchester, NH   Goffstown, NH
Abandoned: 1981   **Railroad:** B&M   **Length:** 8.1   **Opened:** 1850
This segment formed part of the Manchester-Henniker North Weare Branch of the B&M. It was built as the New Hampshire Central RR and in 1853 became part of the Merrimac & Connecticut River RR and later part of the Concord & Montreal RR. The B&M acquired the line in 1895. Passenger service ended in the mid-1930s. Until 1976 the line entered Goffstown via a wooden covered bridge over the Piscataquog River. When the bridge burned, the line was cut back to the river bank. The remainder of the line was taken out of service in 1980.

337

Woodsville, NH   Blackmount, NH
Abandoned: 1981   **Railroad:** B&M   **Length:** 4.3   **Opened:** 1853
This line was built by the Boston, Concord & Montreal, which stretched 94 miles from Concord, NH, to Wells River, VT. For many years the BC&M formed part of a major through route between Boston and Canada. After 1889 this was part of the Concord & Montreal RR and in 1895, the B&M. Passenger service continued until a large portion of the line was abandoned in 1954 (see line 206).

338

Simsbury, CT   Avon, CT
Abandoned: 1981   **Railroad:** CR   **Length:** 5   **Opened:** 1850
The New Haven & Northampton began construction of this part of its main line in 1846 and opened the section between Avon and Simsbury, CT, in 1850. In 1856 the line was extended through Westfield to Northampton, MA. Until 1869 the line was operated under lease to the New York & New Haven RR. After 1869 the line was operated independently until 1887 when it was absorbed into the growing NH system. Passenger service ended around 1928.

338A

Falls Ave. (Milford), MA   Milford, MA
Abandoned: ca. 1981   **Railroad:** CR   **Length:** 0.8   **Opened:** 1872
The Hopkinton RR opened this railroad as part of its line from Ashland to Milford. On completion it was leased to the Providence & Worcester RR, and in 1883 it became part of the Milford & Woonsocket RR. Four years later it was absorbed by the New York & New England RR and in 1898 it became a branch of the NH. Passenger service ended in 1920. In 1953 the I.C.C. authorized abandonment of the line (see line 203), but the NH, the PC, and then Conrail continued to operate this segment.

339

West Kingston, RI   Wakefield, RI
Abandoned: 1981   **Railroad:** NP   **Length:** 5.8   **Opened:** 1876
The NP had been built to service the resort community of Narragansett Pier and textile mills at Peace Dale and Wakefield. Passenger service ended in 1952. The line had been electrified for trolley operation between 1902 and 1920.

340

Aroostook River, ME   West Caribou, ME
Abandoned: 1982   **Railroad:** AV   **Length:** 20.6   **Opened:** 1912
The AV, an electric railroad, built the portion of this line between the Aroostook River (Crouseville) and Washburn in 1910. It completed the line to West Caribou around 1912 or 1913. The AV converted to diesel operation in 1946 and discontinued passenger operations.

341

Collins Siding, ME   Van Buren, ME
Abandoned: 1982   **Railroad:** BAR   **Length:** 10.9   **Opened:** 1899
This segment formed part of the original main line of the BAR. Passenger trains were discontinued in 1960.

342

Ayer, MA   Hollis, NH
Abandoned: 1982   **Railroad:** B&M   **Length:** 11.7   **Opened:** 1848
The Worcester & Nashua RR constructed this line between its namesake cities in 1848. Eventually the line was extended to Rochester, NH, and ultimately to Portland. Renamed the Worcester, Nashua, & Rochester RR in 1883, it became part of the B&M 3 years later. For a time this was a busy main line, but eventually most traffic was routed over other lines. Passenger and freight service ended in 1934. This segment was last used in 1981; the tracks were taken up in 1983-84. The state of Massachusetts acquired the right of way (to the state line) around 1987 and is currently planning to convert in into a bike trail.

342A

Paper Mill Sta., MA   Bradford, MA
Abandoned: 1982   **Railroad:** B&M   **Length:** 1.5   **Opened:** 1851
The Newburyport RR built this line as part of its branch from Georgetown to Haverhill. It became part of the B&M in 1860. Passenger trains last ran in 1933.

343

Rochester, NH   Gonic, NH
Abandoned: 1982   **Railroad:** B&M   **Length:** 0.8   **Opened:** 1849
The Cocheco RR opened this segment as part of its line from Dover to Alton Bay, which it reached in 1851. It passed to the B&M in 1863. Passenger service ended in 1935.

344

Salisbury, MA   Amesbury, MA
Abandoned: 1982   **Railroad:** B&M   **Length:** 3.7   **Opened:** 1848
The Eastern RR built this line as the Salisbury Branch RR, and once completed operated it as its Amesbury Branch. The B&M took over the line in 1884. Passenger service ended in 1936. The line was taken out of service in 1972. The abandoned right of way is now owned by the MBTA.

345

Seabrook, NH   Salisbury, MA
Abandoned: 1982   **Railroad:** B&M   **Length:** 5   **Opened:** 1840
This segment formed part of the original Boston-to-Portsmouth main line of the Eastern RR. The B&M absorbed the Eastern in 1884. Passenger service ended in 1965.

345A

Stoneham, MA   Lindenwood, MA
Abandoned: ca. 1982   **Railroad:** B&M   **Length:** 1.5   **Opened:** 1862
The Boston & Lowell RR built this segment as part of its Stoneham Branch. It was built as the Stoneham Branch RR, but the Boston & Lowell operated the line until 1887, when it became part of the B&M. Passenger service on the branch continued until 1958.

346

Winchester, MA   Woburn, MA
Abandoned: 1982   **Railroad:** B&M   **Length:** 1.8   **Opened:** 1844
The Boston & Lowell RR built this line as its Woburn branch. In 1885 it was extended to connect at both ends with its Boston-Lowell main line. For many years certain Boston-Lowell trains were diverted to serve Woburn. When passenger service finally ended in 1981, the line no longer served any purpose and was abandoned. The MBTA still owns the right of way.

347

Braintree Highlands, MA [1 mi SW]   Randolph, MA [1780 ft SW]
Abandoned: 1982   **Railroad:** CR   **Length:** 1.5   **Opened:** 1866
The Old Colony & Northern built this segment as part of its Dighton & Somerset main line between Braintree Highlands and Fall River. The NH took over operation in 1893. Passenger service ended in 1938.

347A

Wigginville (Lowell), MA   Rogers St. (Lowell), MA
Abandoned: 1982   **Railroad:** B&M   **Length:** 1   **Opened:** 1874
In 1874 the B&M challenged Boston & Lowell's monopoly on providing rail service to Lowell by constructing a branch from its main line at Lowell Jct. to a station in downtown

Lowell on Central St. (still standing). This branch formed part of that line. In 1887, however, the B&M acquired the Boston & Lowell, and it no longer had need for two Lowell stations. A connection between the Lowell Branch and the ex-Boston & Lowell main line was made at the Bleachery, and passenger service on this segment ended in 1895. The tracks between Rogers St. and the station (about 2000 feet) were removed around 1950, but this segment continued in use through the 1970s.

347B

Chelmsford, MA   South Chelmsford, MA
Abandoned: 1982   **Railroad:** CR   **Length:** 2.4   **Opened:** 1871
This segment once formed part of the main line of the Framingham & Lowell RR. In 1879 it became part of the Old Colony RR system and in 1893 a branch of the New Haven. Passenger service ceased in 1933, but throughout the NH period it was used for through freight trains out of northern New England via the B&M at Lowell. These became less frequent once the PC took over the NH in 1969. In 1976, this segment was not included in the former PC lines taken over by Conrail, but Conrail was paid by the state to operate the line for a few more years. When the subsidy ended, the line was abandoned. Some of the track remains in place. The state owns the right of way and plans to convert it into a bike trail.

348

Indian Orchard, MA   Ludlow, MA
Abandoned: 1982   **Railroad:** CR   **Length:** 0.9   **Opened:** 1873
The Springfield, Athol & Northeastern RR built this line as part of its through route between Athol and Springfield. The B&A took over the Springfield, Athol & Northeastern in 1880 and operated it as its Athol Branch. Passenger service ended in 1935.

349

Livermore Falls, ME   Farmington, ME
Abandoned: 1982   **Railroad:** MC   **Length:** 16.1   **Opened:** 1859
The broad-gauge Androscoggin RR got underway in 1850 heading north from Leeds Jct. By 1852 it reached Livermore Falls, North Jay by 1856, East Wilton by 1857, and Farmington in 1859. The Adroscoggin was reorganized as the Leeds & Farmington RR in 1865 but continued to be operated by the Androscoggin. It was absorbed by the MC in 1874. Passenger service was provided as late as 1956. The old right of way between Jay and Farmington today is used by the Jay to Farmington Trail.

350

at West Cambridge, MA
Abandoned: 1983   **Railroad:** B&M   **Length:** 1.1
This was apparently yard trackage in West Cambridge. The last shipper no longer needed service and part of the right of way was used for a highway project.

350A

East Northfield, MA   Brattleboro, VT
Abandoned: 1983   **Railroad:** B&M   **Length:** 11.3   **Opened:** 1912
The portion of this line from East Northfield to Dole Jct., NH, was completed by the Ashuelot RR in 1851. This eventually became part of the B&M in 1893. Around 1912 the

B&M constructed a line between Dole Jct. and Brattleboro, so that the railroad no longer had to use the parallel tracks of the CV along the opposite bank of the Connecticut River.

350B

Dole Jct., NH   Keene, NH
Abandoned: 1983   **Railroad:** B&M   **Length:** 21.7   **Opened:** 1851
The Ashuelot RR completed its line between East Northfield, MA, and Keene, NH in 1851. The Connecticut River RR operated the line to 1860, when it became part of the Cheshire RR system. The Connecticut River recovered the line in 1877 and continued to operate it until it was absorbed by the B&M in 1893. Passenger service ended in 1958. The Green Mountain RR obtained trackage rights over the Ashuelot Branch in 1977, and became the sole operator afterwards. When the Green Mountain discontinued operation of the line in 1983 the B&M, who still owned the branch, was permitted to abandon it.

350C

at Keene, NH
Abandoned: 1983   **Railroad:** B&M   **Length:** 3.1   **Opened:** 1849
This segment, which consisted of yard trackage in Keene, once formed part of the main line of the Cheshire RR, which stretched from South Ashburnham, MA, to Bellows Falls, VT. The entire line was completed in 1849. The Cheshire acquired other small railroads and operated independently until 1890 when it became part of the Fitchburg RR system. In 1900 the B&M absorbed the Fitchburg. In the first half of the twentieth century this was a major passenger route between Boston and Montreal via Fitchburg, Bellows Falls, and Rutland. When the Rutland RR ended all passenger service on its Vermont lines in 1953, the line was deprived of most of its passenger traffic, and passenger service ended in 1958. The subsequent collapse of the Rutland RR in the early 1960s further reduced freight traffic. In 1977 the Green Mountain RR began operating this track as an extension of the Ashuelot Branch, but when it ended this operation in 1983, the B&M was permitted to abandon the line.

351

Mount Tom, MA   Easthampton, MA
Abandoned: 1983   **Railroad:** B&M   **Length:** 3.4   **Opened:** 1872
The Connecticut River RR built its Easthampton Branch in 1872. It ultimately became a B&M branch in 1893. Passenger service was discontinued around 1926.

352

Salem, NH   Derry, NH
Abandoned: 1983   **Railroad:** B&M   **Length:** 9   **Opened:** 1849
The Manchester & Lawrence built this segment as part of its main line between its namesake cities. The Concord RR gained control in 1850 and operated the line until 1870, when it became a branch of the Northern RR. The B&M absorbed the line in 1887. Regular passenger service ended in 1953.

352A

Wamesit, MA   Tewksbury Centre, MA
Abandoned: ca. 1983   **Railroad:** B&M   **Length:** 1   **Opened:** 1848
This segment once formed part of the Lowell & Lawrence RR, which connected these two industrial cities. The Boston & Lowell RR acquired this line in 1858 and in 1887 it

became a branch of the B&M. The B&M had no real need for two routes between Lowell and Lawrence, but it did not get around to abandoning the bulk of the Lowell & Lawrence until 1926 (passenger service ended 1924). This short segment survived as a freight branch serving a few industrial customers until around 1979.

353

Montville, CT   Palmerton, CT
Abandoned: 1983   **Railroad:** CV   **Length:** 2.6   **Opened:** 1899
This freight-only branch was built by the CV to serve some industries in Palmerton. It continued in use until 1981 when it was closed on account of flood damage.

354

Pittsfield, ME   Hartland, ME
Abandoned: 1983   **Railroad:** MC   **Length:** 8.6   **Opened:** 1886
The Sebasticook & Moosehead Lake RR had great ambitions in the 1880s, but it only managed to build a 17-mile branch line between Pittsfield and Harmony. It became part of the MC in 1911. Passenger service was discontinued in 1938 or 1939.

354A

East Braintree, MA   West Hingham, MA
Abandoned: 1983   **Railroad:** CR   **Length:** 5.2   **Opened:** 1849
The South Shore RR opened this line in 1849. For a few years the Old Colony RR operated it, but for more than 20 years the line ran independently. The Old Colony took over the line in 1877, and was absorbed by the NH in 1893. Between 1898 and 1906 the line was electrified using a third rail. Passenger service continued over this line until the discontinuation of all Old Colony commuter routes in 1959. The line carried little freight and was abandoned. Today the MBTA and the state are seeking to rebuild the line to reintroduce rail commuter service to Greenbush.

355

Bridgewater, ME   Phair, ME
Abandoned: 1984   **Railroad:** BAR   **Length:** 17.3   **Opened:** 1895
This line formed part of what originally was the BAR main line. Passenger service ended in 1961.

356

Chicopee Center, MA   Chicopee Falls, MA
Abandoned: 1984   **Railroad:** B&M   **Length:** 1.4   **Opened:** 1845
The Connecticut River RR built this segment as part of its Chicopee Falls Branch at the same time as it constructed its main line. After many years of operation by the Connecticut River, the line became a B&M branch in 1893. Passenger service ended in 1918. At the time of abandonment the line had been out of service for more than 2 years.

357

West Concord, NH   Concord, NH
Abandoned: 1984   **Railroad:** B&M   **Length:** 1.1   **Opened:** 1848
The Concord & Claremont RR built this line. It was merged with other lines to form the New Hampshire Central RR in 1853. It became the C&C once more in 1873, but eventually passed to the B&M in 1887. In 1954 the B&M turned over the remainder of

the old C&C to a new Claremont & Concord RR, but retained this line. The line was out of service by 1982.

358

South Ashburnham, MA [0.7 mi W]   Jaffrey, NH
Abandoned: 1984   **Railroad:** B&M   **Length:** 20.6   **Opened:** 1870
This line was built as two segments. The tracks between South Ashburnham and Winchendon once formed part of the main line of the Cheshire RR. The Vermont & Massachusetts (later Fitchburg) RR was once planned to pass through Winchendon, but before this part of the main line could be completed, it was relocated through Gardner instead. The Vermont & Massachusetts therefore sold this now unneeded main line to the Cheshire RR, who completed it in 1847 and by 1849 had extended it to Bellows Falls. Ultimately it formed part of a through route to Montreal. The segment between Winchendon and Jaffrey was built in 1870 by the Monadnock RR as part of its line to Peterborough. In 1880 the Cheshire took over the Monadnock, and in 1890 the Fitchburg absorbed both. Ten years later the B&M acquired the entire Fitchburg system. Passenger service between Winchendon and Jaffrey ended in 1953 and between Ashburnham and Winchendon in 1958. The track was removed in 1986.

359

at Calais, ME
Abandoned: 1984   **Railroad:** MC   **Length:** 0.8   **Opened:** 1898
This line was built as part of the Washington County RR, which stretched from the border at Calais to Ellsworth. It became part of the MC in 1904. The line had been out of service more than 2 years at the time of its abandonment.

360

at Lewiston, ME
Abandoned: 1984   **Railroad:** MC   **Length:** 0.6   **Opened:** 1861
This formed the end of the Lewiston Lower Branch, a standard-gauge extension of the then broad-gauge Androscoggin RR that connected Lewiston with Crowley Jct. Passenger service ceased around 1933.

361

East Deerfield (Deerfield Jct.), MA   Turners Falls, MA
Abandoned: 1985   **Railroad:** B&M   **Length:** 3.7   **Opened:** 1882
The New Haven & Northampton RR built this branch, which closely paralleled an existing line of the Fitchburg RR. The NH took over the line in 1887. Passenger service ended around 1919. In 1947 the NH sold this line to the B&M, which had been using it in place of its own branch (the old Fitchburg branch). It was last used in 1982.

361A

North Windham, CT   Willimantic, CT
Abandoned: ca. 1985   **Railroad:** P&W   **Length:** 5   **Opened:** 1872
The Boston, Hartford & Erie RR opened this segment in 1872 as part of its Boston-to-Providence/New Haven main line. It became a component of the New York & New England RR in 1875 and ultimately part of the NH in 1898. Daily Boston-Hartford passenger trains used the route until August 1955 when severe floods destroyed a bridge near Putnam and took the line out of service. Passenger service never resumed. The ICC

authorized the abandonment of this segment in 1963 (see line 248), but the line remained in service into the 1980s, the final provider being the P&W.

363

Brewer, ME   St. Croix Jct. (Calais), ME

Abandoned: 1985   **Railroad:** MC   **Length:** 126.9   **Opened:** 1898

This segment, the longest line abandoned at one time in New England, was constructed by two different railroads. The section between Brewer and Washington Jct. (near Ellsworth) was built by the Maine Shore RR, a subsidiary of the MC, in 1883. The Washington County RR began at Washington Jct. and completed the line to Calais in 1898. In 1904 the MC took over operation of the Washington County and now operated both lines as one (formal merger came in 1911). Passenger service continued until the end of all MC passenger operations in 1960. Ten years after the abandonment some or most of the tracks remain, although grade crossings have been paved over.

364

Collins Siding, ME   Blackstone Siding, ME

Abandoned: 1986   **Railroad:** BAR   **Length:** 11.7   **Opened:** 1910

The Collins-to-Stockholm portion of this line was completed in 1899, and the rest of the line in 1910. Passenger service between Stockholm and Collins lasted until 1960, but service on the section from Stockholm to Blackstone had ended in the 1950s.

365

Dover, NH   Sawyer, NH

Abandoned: 1986   **Railroad:** B&M   **Length:** 1.4   **Opened:** 1874

The Eastern RR leased the Portsmouth & Dover RR as soon as the latter had completed its 11-mile line between its namesake cities in 1874. The B&M took over a decade later. Passenger service ended in January 1933.

366

Derry, NH   Grenier AFB (Londonderry), NH

Abandoned: 1986   **Railroad:** B&M   **Length:** 4.9   **Opened:** 1849

The Manchester & Lawrence built this segment as part of its main line between its namesake cities. The Concord RR gained control in 1850 and operated the line until 1870, when it became a branch of the Northern RR. The B&M absorbed the line in 1887. Regular passenger service ended in 1953.

368

Manchester, CT   South Manchester, CT

Abandoned: 1986   **Railroad:** CR   **Length:** 2   **Opened:** 1869

The South Manchester RR was built by the Cheney family, who owned the silk mills in South Manchester. For many years this two-mile long railroad was operated independently, but in 1933 the NH finally took over the line. Passenger service ended at this time. Service on the line was suspended in 1981.

369

South Windsor, CT   East Windsor, CT
Abandoned: ca. 1986   **Railroad:** CR   **Length:** 6.8   **Opened:** 1876
This line was part of the Connecticut Central RR, which opened its line between Hartford and Springfield in 1876. At first the line was operated by the Connecticut Valley RR under lease (as a logical extension of its Old Saybrook-Hartford main line), but it soon was canceled, leaving the Connecticut Central to operate on its own until 1880 when it was leased to the New York & New England RR. The NH took over in 1898. Passenger service ended around 1931.

371

at Burlington, VT
Abandoned: 1986   **Railroad:** VT   **Length:** 1.8   **Opened:** 1899
The Rutland RR built this line as part of its route across the islands of Lake Champlain in 1899 to give it a direct line to Rouses Point and Canada independent of the CV. It was built as the Rutland-Canada RR but always operated as part of the Rutland. Passenger service ended in 1953. It was last operated in 1961, and was abandoned along with the entire Rutland RR. The Vermont RY reopened this line in 1964 but discontinued operations again in 1975.

372

Sanbornville, NH   Wolfeboro, NH
Abandoned: 1986   **Railroad:** WOLF   **Length:** 12   **Opened:** 1872
Built as the Wolfeborough RR, this line was leased to the Eastern RR before completion. The B&M took over from the Eastern in 1884. The B&M discontinued passenger service around 1938 and by 1972 was planning to abandon the line. Instead the B&M sold the line to a new Wolfeboro RR who operated it as a tourist excursion line with steam locomotives hauling passenger trains. Unfortunately, the operation was unsuccessful and closed down.

373

New Haven, CT   Cheshire, CT
Abandoned: 1987   **Railroad:** B&M   **Length:** 14.8   **Opened:** 1847
The New Haven & Northampton RR was built along the path of the Farmington Canal (completed 1835). Much of the rail line between New Haven and Hamden, however, originally ran alongside or even on the old Cheshire Turnpike (it was relocated to the present right of way in 1880). Between 1848 and 1869 the New Haven & Northampton was leased to the New York & New Haven RR. After 1869 independent operation resumed until 1887 when it became part of the NH system. Passenger service ended around 1928. In 1969 the PC took over the line and was succeeded by Conrail in 1976. The B&M took over operation of the segment in 1982 but soon ended service.

374

West Peabody, MA   South Middleton, MA
Abandoned: 1987   **Railroad:** B&M   **Length:** 3.6   **Opened:** 1850
This was part of the Salem & Lowell RR's main line between its namesake cities. It was operated first by the Lowell & Lawrence RR and after 1858 by the Boston & Lowell. It became a branch of the B&M in 1887. Passenger service ended in 1932.

375

Cochituate, MA   Saxonville, MA
Abandoned: ca. 1987   **Railroad:** CR   **Length:** 1.5   **Opened:** 1846
This segment forms the outermost part of the Saxonville Branch of the old Boston & Worcester RR. It became a branch of the B&A in 1867, the PC in 1968, and ultimately CR in 1976. Passenger service was discontinued in 1936.

376

Pleasant St. (Claremont), NH   Washington St. (Claremont), NH
Abandoned: 1988   **Railroad:** C&C   **Length:** 1.5   **Opened:** 1872
The Sugar River RR built this line as an extension of the Concord & Claremont RR. It became part of the C&C in 1873, but eventually passed to the B&M in 1887. In 1954 the line was sold to a new Claremont & Concord RR. Passenger service ended the year following.

376A

Claremont, NH   West Claremont, NH
Abandoned: 1988   **Railroad:** C&C   **Length:** 3   **Opened:** 1903
An electric railroad, the Claremont RY, put this line in service in 1903. Passenger service ceased in 1930, but freight continued to be carried under the wires until around 1955 when the line was taken over by the Claremont & Concord RR. Diesel power was then used on the line until abandonment.

377

Albertson, VT   West Rutland, VT
Abandoned: 1988   **Railroad:** C&P   **Length:** 2   **Opened:** 1903
This extension of the C&P was built around 1903 to reach a quarry. Rock was the principal commodity of the C&P.

377A

at Rutland, VT
Abandoned: 1988   **Railroad:** C&P   **Length:** 1   **Opened:** 1886
The C&P built this as part of its line between Center Rutland and West Rutland. It was primarily used to haul rock from local quarries.

378

at Portland, ME
Abandoned: 1988   **Railroad:** CN   **Length:** 2.2   **Opened:** 1853
This was the initial two miles of the Atlantic & St. Lawrence RR. Construction on this broad gauge line to Montreal began in 1846. The Grand Trunk Railway leased the line as soon as it was constructed. It was converted to standard gauge in 1874. In 1923 the CN took over operation of the Grand Trunk. Passenger service to Portland lasted until 1960. This line had been out of operation since 1984 when its bridge across the harbor was closed.

379

Houlton, ME   Canadian border
Abandoned: 1989   **Railroad:** CP   **Length:** 3   **Opened:** 1862
The New Brunswick & Canada RR constructed this short international branch line in the 1860s. It became part of the New Brunswick RY in 1882 before becoming a CP branch line. Passenger service ended in 1949.

380

Presque Isle, ME   Canadian border
Abandoned: 1989   **Railroad:** CP   **Length:** 26.8   **Opened:** 1881
The Aroostook River RR, a 3½ foot gauge line, constructed this line, which by the time it was completed had been leased to the New Brunswick RY. By the time it became a CP branch in 1890 it had been converted to standard gauge. Passenger service was discontinued around 1939. At the time of abandonment it was already out of service.

381

Pittsfield city line, MA   Adams, MA
Abandoned: 1990   **Railroad:** B&M   **Length:** 10.5   **Opened:** 1846
Although built by the Pittsfield & North Adams RR, this line was always operated as a branch of the Western (later B&A) RR. Passenger service ended in 1953. In 1968 the line became a branch of the PC and after 1976, CR. In 1981 the B&M took over operation. Service on this segment ceased in 1988. The rails were lifted in 1993 and 1994. The state has acquired the right of way for possible conversion to a recreational trail.

382

Sheldon Jct., VT   St. Albans, VT
Abandoned: 1990   **Railroad:** CV   **Length:** 9.4   **Opened:** 1871
This line once formed part of the Missisquoi RR, which by the time it was completed had been leased to the Vermont Central RR. Two years later that railroad was renamed the CV. The bondholders of the line took back control in 1877 and operated this independently until the CV again leased the line in 1886. Passenger service ended in 1938 or 1939. Prior to abandonment this line had been out of service since 1984, when a wreck damaged a bridge at Sheldon Jct.

384

Dover-Foxcroft, ME   Newport, ME
Abandoned: 1990   **Railroad:** MC   **Length:** 29.3   **Opened:** 1889
The Dexter & Newport RR opened a line between Newport and Dexter in 1869 and turned the line over to the MC. In 1889 the MC, under a charter for the Dexter & Piscataquis RR, extended it to Dover-Foxcroft. Passenger trains last operated around 1933. The line had been taken out of service by 1986. The state acquired the right of way in 1995 for use as a recreational trail.

384A

Dexter St. (Cumberland), RI   Valley Falls, RI
Abandoned: 1990   **Railroad:** P&W   **Length:** 0.9   **Opened:** 1877
This line was built in 1877 as part of the Franklin, MA-Valley Falls branch of the New York & New England RR, though technically it was built by the Rhode Island & Massachusetts

RR. Passenger service, which once included some Boston-Providence trains, ceased in 1938.

385

Providence, RI   Coventry (Washington), RI
Abandoned: 1990   **Railroad:** P&W   **Length:** 14.6   **Opened:** 1854
This line once formed part of the Hartford, Providence & Fishkill RR. By 1855 the tracks were completed 122 miles from Providence to Waterbury. The New York & New England RR absorbed the line in 1878, and 20 years later it passed to the NH. Passenger service ended around 1932.

386

Washburn, ME   Blackstone Siding (Westmoreland), ME
Abandoned: 1991   **Railroad:** BAR   **Length:** 15.9   **Opened:** 1910
At time of abandonment this line, which once formed part of the BAR's cutoff from Squa Pan to Stockholm, had been out of service for at least 2 years. Passenger service had been reduced to mixed train service by 1951 and was discontinued a few years later.

387

Boscowen, NH   Lebanon, NH
Abandoned: 1992   **Railroad:** B&M   **Length:** 59.3   **Opened:** 1847
The Northern RR built this segment as part of its main line between Concord, NH, and White River Jct, VT. It became part of one of the most important Boston-Montreal routes. Absorbed by the Boston & Lowell, it became a B&M line in 1887. Passenger service survived until 1965. The tracks between Boscowen and Franklin were lifted in 1992; the rails as far as Canaan were gone by the end of 1994.

388

Plainville, CT   Avon, CT
Abandoned: 1991   **Railroad:** B&M   **Length:** 8.2   **Opened:** 1850
The New Haven & Northampton began construction of this part of its main line in 1846 and opened this section in 1850. In 1856 the line was extended through Westfield to Northampton, MA. Until 1869 the line was operated under lease to the New York & New Haven RR. After 1869 the line was operated independently until 1887 when it was absorbed into the growing NH system. Passenger service ended around 1928. Between 1969 and 1976 the line was part of the PC, and afterwards, a branch of CR. In 1982 operation was taken over by the B&M.

389A

Saylesville, RI   Pawtucket city line, RI
Abandoned: 1991   **Railroad:** P&W   **Length:** 1   **Opened:** 1877
This line was built by the Moshassuck Valley RR as part of its 2-mile route. The Moshassuck Valley, despite its diminutive size, retained its independence for more than a century. Passenger service was discontinued in 1921. The Moshassuck Valley finally was sold to the P&W in 1982, which operated it as its Moshassuck Industrial Track.

390

South Auburn, RI   Pontiac, RI
Abandoned: 1991   **Railroad:** P&W   **Length:** 3.9   **Opened:** 1880
This line was built by the New York, Providence & Boston RR to form a through line between Auburn and Hope. The NH acquired the line in 1892. Passenger trains last ran in 1922. The PC took over operation of the line from the NH in 1969. In 1976 the P&W obtained the line and operated it as its Pontiac Secondary Track.

391

Charleston, NH   Springfield, VT
Abandoned: 1991   **Railroad:** ST   **Length:** 3.9   **Opened:** 1897
Built by the Springfield Electric RY as a trolley line, this railroad was reorganized as the ST in 1923. It included the Cheshire Bridge, an old toll bridge that the trolley shared with road vehicles and which generated much revenue for the railway. Springfield, a busy factory town, produced considerable freight traffic. Passenger service continued until 1947, and electric freight service was provided until 1956, when it was converted to diesel operation. By the mid-1980s the line was out of service.

392

West Somerville, MA   Somerville, MA
Abandoned: 1992   **Railroad:** B&M   **Length:** 1   **Opened:** 1870
The Boston & Lowell RR constructed this line after it purchased control of the Lexington & Arlington RR in 1870. It thus connected that railroad with the Boston & Lowell main line in Somerville. In 1887 it became part of the B&M. In 1926 passenger trains from the Lexington & Arlington Branch were rerouted over the Fitchburg line and this became part of the B&M's freight cutoff. Most B&M freight trains headed in or out of Boston used this line until 1979, when the B&M abandoned the line west of this segment so that part of the right of way could be used by the MBTA to extend its Red Line transit to Alewife Brook station. Only local freights used this segment afterwards.

393

New Britain, CT   Elmwood, CT
Abandoned: 1992   **Railroad:** B&M   **Length:** 5.9   **Opened:** 1850
This line once formed part of the Providence-Hartford-Waterbury main line of the Hartford, Providence & Fishkill RR. In 1878 it became part of the New York & New England RR, and after 1898 was part of the NH. Passenger service ended in 1959. The PC succeeded the NH in 1969 and in 1976 the line passed to CR. The B&M took over operation of the line in 1982. By 1990 the line was out of service, with remaining traffic rerouted over the closely parallel Amtrak New Haven-Springfield line and the New Britain Branch.

394

Sheldon Jct., VT   Richford, VT
Abandoned: 1992   **Railroad:** CV   **Length:** 17.4   **Opened:** 1872
This line once formed part of the Missisquoi RR, which by the time it was completed, had been leased to the Vermont Central RR, Two years later that railroad was renamed the

CV. Passenger service ended in 1938 or 1939. This line had been out of service since 1984, when a bridge at Sheldon Jct. suffered damage in a wreck.

395

Presque Isle Jct., ME   Dyer St. (Presque Isle), ME
Abandoned: 1993   **Railroad:** AV   **Length:** 1.7   **Opened:** 1910
The AV, an electric railroad, built this line in 1910. The AV converted to diesel operation in 1946 and discontinued passenger operations.

396

Washburn Jct., ME   Aroostook River, ME
Abandoned: 1993   **Railroad:** AV   **Length:** 3   **Opened:** 1910
Part of the same route as line 395; see the note for that segment.

396A

Adams, MA   Renfrew, MA
Abandoned: 1994   **Railroad:** B&M   **Length:** 1   **Opened:** 1846
Although built by the Pittsfield & North Adams RR, this line was always operated as a branch of the Western (later B&A) RR. Passenger service ended in 1953. In 1968 the line became a branch of the PC and after 1976, CR. In 1981 the B&M took over operation of the line. It was out of service at the time of abandonment. The rails were taken up in 1995.

397

Chicopee, MA   Chicopee Center, MA
Abandoned: 1993   **Railroad:** B&M   **Length:** 0.8   **Opened:** 1845
The Connecticut River RR built this segment as part of its Chicopee Falls Branch at the same time as it constructed its main line. After many years of operation by the Connecticut River, the line became a B&M branch in 1893. Passenger service ended in 1918. At the time of abandonment the line had been out of service for more than 2 years.

398

at Nashua, NH
Abandoned: 1993   **Railroad:** B&M   **Length:** 1.6   **Opened:** 1848
This segment formed the first 1.6 miles out of Nashua of the old Worcester & Nashua RR, which was constructed between its namesake cities in 1848. Eventually the line was extended to Rochester, NH., and ultimately to Portland. Renamed the Worcester, Nashua, & Rochester RR in 1883, it became part of the B&M 3 years later. For a time this was a busy main line, but eventually most traffic was routed over other lines. Passenger and through freight service ended in 1934. This short segment continued to serve a few local industries until the late 1980s.

399

Castle Hill (Salem), MA   Loring Ave. (Salem), MA
Abandoned: 1993   **Railroad:** B&M   **Length:** 0.8   **Opened:** 1839
This segment formed the final remnant of what once was a branch line to Marblehead. It was built along with the original Eastern RR from Boston to Newburyport, and it became another B&M branch in 1884. Passenger trains continued until 1959. At the time of abandonment it had not been used for more than 2 years.

400

at South Ashburnham, MA
Abandoned: 1993   **Railroad:** B&M   **Length:** 0.7   **Opened:** 1847
This segment once formed part of the main line of the Cheshire RR. The Vermont & Massachusetts (later Fitchburg) RR was once planned to pass through Winchendon, but before this part of the main line could be completed, it was rerouted through Gardner instead. The Vermont & Massachusetts therefore sold this now unneeded main line to the Cheshire RR, who completed it in 1847 and by 1849 had extended it to Bellows Falls. Ultimately it formed part of a through route to Montreal. In 1890 the Fitchburg absorbed the Cheshire, and ten years later the B&M acquired the entire Fitchburg system. Passenger service ended in 1958. By the time of abandonment this line was out of service.

401

Springfield, MA   Hazardville, CT
Abandoned: 1993   **Railroad:** B&M   **Length:** 12.5   **Opened:** 1876
This line was part of the Connecticut Central RR, which opened its line between Hartford and Springfield in 1876. At first the line was operated by the Connecticut Valley RR under lease (as a logical extension of its Old Saybrook-Hartford main line), but it soon was canceled, leaving the Connecticut Central to operate on its own until 1880 when it was leased to the New York & New England RR. The NH took over in 1898. Passenger service ended around 1933. The PC assumed operation of the line in 1969 and in 1976 it became a CR branch line. In 1982 the B&M began operating the line as its Armory Branch, and this continued until operation ceased in 1990.

402

Waltham North, MA   Clematis Brook, MA
Abandoned: 1994   **Railroad:** B&M   **Length:** 1.5   **Opened:** 1881
This segment was virtually the last surviving remnant of the Boston-Northampton main line of the Massachusetts Central (Central Massachusetts) RR. The Boston & Lowell RR eventually took over operation of the line in 1886, and in turn passed it to the B&M in 1887. Passenger service out of Boston was provided on the entire segment until 1958, when Hudson became the terminus. After 1965 the trains went no farther than South Sudbury. Passenger service ended altogether in 1971.

403

at Waterbury, CT
Abandoned: 1994   **Railroad:** B&M   **Length:** 2.6   **Opened:** 1888
This was a remnant of the Meriden, Waterbury & Connecticut RR. It became part of the New York & New England in 1892. Not operated between 1896 and 1898, it became a seldom-used line of the New Haven. Passenger service ended in 1917. Operated by PC and later CR, it became a B&M/Guilford branch in the 1980s. The line was out of service by the early 1990s.

404

at Lowell, MA
Abandoned: 1994   **Railroad:** B&M   **Length:** 0.8   **Opened:** 1871
This segment once formed part of the main line of the Framingham & Lowell RR. In 1879 it became part of the Old Colony RR system and in 1893 a branch of the New Haven.

Passenger service ceased in 1933, but throughout the NH period it was used for through freight trains out of northern New England via the B&M at Lowell. These became less frequent once the PC took over the NH in 1969. In 1976 this segment, isolated from the rest of the CR system, was transferred to the B&M. It was last used around 1991 to store freight cars.

405

Lindenwood, MA   Montvale, MA
Abandoned: 1994   **Railroad:** B&M   **Length:** 0.9   **Opened:** 1862
The Boston & Lowell RR built this segment as part of its Stoneham Branch. Although it was built as the Stoneham Branch RR, the Boston & Lowell operated the line until 1887, when it became part of the B&M. Passenger service on the branch continued until 1958. The MBTA now owns the abandoned right of way.

406

Ipswich, MA   Newburyport, MA
Abandoned: 1994   **Railroad:** B&M   **Length:** 9.5   **Opened:** 1840
Built by the Eastern RR as part of its Boston-Portsmouth-Portland main line, this became a part of the B&M in 1884. Passenger service lasted until 1976. The line was last used in 1984. This abandonment may prove to be temporary, since the MBTA, which owns the right of way, is considering the restoration of commuter rail service to Newburyport.

407

Westbrook, ME   State Line (Fryeburg), ME
Abandoned: 1994   **Railroad:** MC   **Length:** 43.4   **Opened:** 1875
The Portland & Ogdensburg RR constructed this line as part of its route between Portland and Lunenburg, VT. The MC took over operation of the line in 1888 and it formed part of the latter's Mountain Division. Passenger service was discontinued in 1958. The line was taken out of service in 1983.

Bibliography

Adams, Robert B. "Born and Buried in Six Months [Billerica & Bedford RR]." *Trains*, September 1959, 34-39.

Andrews, Richard. "From Randolph to Togus on the Kennebec Central." *Trains*, September 1951, 24-26.

Andrews, Richard L. "Old 2x6 [Monson RR]." *Trains & Travel*, May 1953, 28-30.

Angier, Jerry, and Herb Cleaves. *Bangor and Aroostook: The Maine Railroad.* Littleton, Mass.: Flying Yankee, 1986.

Armstrong, Jack. *Railfan's Guide to New England.* Adams, Mass.: Armstrong, 1987.

Baker, George Pierce. *The Formation of the New England Railroad Systems: A Study of Railroad Combination in the Nineteenth Century.* Cambridge: Harvard University Press, 1937.

Biondi, Arnold S., and Frederick W. Lyman. *Abandoned Railroads in Maine: Their Potential for Trail Use.* Augusta: Maine Dept. of Parks and Recreation, 1973.

The Central Mass. N.p.: Boston & Maine Railroad Historical Society, 1975.

Blackwell, Walter. *Tracing the Route of the Martha's Vineyard Railroad, 1874-1896.* Miami: Englehart Printing Co., 1971.

Bradlee, Francis B. C. *The Boston and Lowell Railroad, the Nashua and Lowell Railroad, and the Salem and Lowell Railroad.* Salem, Mass.: Essex Institute, 1918.

Bradlee, Francis B. C. *The Boston and Maine Railroad: A History of the Main Route with its Tributary Lines.* Salem, Mass.: Essex Institute, 1921.

Brown, C. A. "The Unused Hampden Railroad." *Shoreliner* 22 (no. 1, 1991): 6-15.

Brown, C. A. "Wood River Branch." *Shoreliner* 19 (no. 3, 1988): 30-39.

Carman, Barnard R. *Hoot, Toot & Whistle: The Story of the Hoosac Tunnel & Wilmington Railroad*. Brattleboro, Vt.: Stephen Green Press, 1963.

The Central Mass. N.p.: Boston & Maine Railroad Historical Society, 1975.

Chase, Edward E. *Maine Railroads: A History of the Development of the Maine Railroad System*. Portland, Me.: Chase, 1926.

Cherington, Charles R. *The Regulation of Railroad Abandonments*. Cambridge: Harvard University Press, 1948.

Chronological History of the New Haven Railroad. N.p.: New Haven Railroad Athletic Association, [1952?].

Connecticut Department of Transportation, Office of Transport Systems. *Connecticut Today: Vol. 4, Rail Transportation System*. Hartford: 1980.

Cornwall, L. Peter, and Carol A. Smith. *Names First–Rails Later*. Stamford, Conn.: Arden Valley Group, 1989.

Crittenden, H. Temple. *The Maine Scenic Route: A History of the Sandy River & Rangeley Lakes Railroad*. Parsons, W.V.: McLain, 1966.

Crittenden, H. Temple. "A Wonderful Little Railroad [Sandy River & Rangeley Lakes RR]." *Trains*, October 1965, 37-51.

Crouch, H. Bentley, and R. Richard Conard. "The Central Mass. Revisited." *B&M Bulletin* 14 (December 1985): 17-24.

Crouch, H. Bentley, and Harry A.Frye. "Worcester, Nashua & Portland: Part 1, The "Phantom" Division; Part 3, All Those Branches." *B&M Bulletin* 9 (Summer 1979): 5-14; (Winter 1979-80): 21-33.

Day, Richard L. *Aroostook Valley Railroad Company*. Bulletin 65. Chicago: Central Electric Railfans' Association, 1946.

Della Penna, Craig. *Great Rail-Trails of the Northeast: The Essential Outdoor Guide to 26 Recreational-Biking Trails and Their Railroad History*. Amherst, Mass.: New England Cartographics, 1995.

Gamst, Frederick C. "The Context and Significance of America´s First Railroad, on Boston's Beacon Hill." <I>Technology & Culture<D> 33 (1992): 66-100.

Greene, J. R. *The Hampden Railroad: A Reprint of a 1913 Article with Historical Notes*. Athol: Transcript Press, 1992.

Harbridge House, Inc. *Availability and Use of Abandoned Rights of Way: Task 2, Inventory of Abandoned Rights of Way, Pursuant to Section 809(a) of the Railroad Revitalization and Regulatory Reform Act*. Washington, D.C.: U.S. Department of Transportation, 1977.

Harlow, Alvin F. *Steelways of New England*. New York: Creative Age Press, 1946.

Henwood, James N. S. *Short Haul to the Bay: A History of the Naragansett Pier Railroad*. Brattleboro, Vt.: Stephen Greene Press, 1969.

Hilton, George W., and John F. Due. *The Electric Interurban Railways in America*. Stanford: Stanford University Press, 1960.

Hoisington, Richard A., and E. Robert Hornsby. "The Amesbury and Merrimac Branches–And Never the Trains Shall Meet." 2 pts. *B&M Bulletin* 10 (Spring 1981): 19-26; (Summer 1981): 7-12.

Humphrey, Thomas J., and Norton D.Clark. *Boston's Commuter Rail: Second Section*. BSRA Bulletin 20. Cambridge, Mass.: Boston Street Railway Association, 1986.

Humphrey, Thomas J., and Norton D.Clark. *Boston's Commuter Rail: The First 150 Years*. BSRA Bulletin 19. Cambridge, Mass.: Boston Street Railway Association, 1985.

Jacobs, Warren. "Story of the New England [New York & New England RR]." *Railway and Locomotive Historical Society Bulletin* , No. 1 (1921): 13-18.

Jones, Robert C. *The Central Vermont Railway: A Yankee Tradition*. 6 vols. Silverton, Colo.: Sundance, 1981.

Jones, Robert C. *Railroads of Vermont*. 2 vols. Shelburne, Vt.: New England Press, 1993.

Jones, Robert C., Whitney J. Maxfield, and William C. Gove. *Vermont's Granite Railroads: The Montpelier & Wells River and the Barre & Chelsea*. Boulder, Col.: Pruett, 1985.

Judkins, Harold I. "I Remember Reformatory Station." *B&M Bulletin* 9 (Spring 1980): 25.

Karr, Ronald Dale. *The Rail Lines of Southern New England: A Handbook of Railroad History*. Pepperell, Mass.: Branch Line Press, 1995.

Keilty, Edmund. *Doodlebug Country: The Rail Motorcar on the Class 1 Railroads of the United States*. Glendale, Calif.: Interurban Press, 1982.

Kirkland, Edward Chase. *Men, Cities and Transportation: A Study in New England History, 1820-1900*. 2 vols. Cambridge: Harvard University Press, 1948.

Kyper, Frank. *The Railroad that Came Out at Night: A Book of Railroading in and around Boston*. Brattleboro, Vt.: Stephen Greene Press, 1977.

Lancaster, Clay. *The Far-Out Island Railroad: Nantucket's Old Summer Narrow Gauge, 1879-1918*. Nantucket, Mass.: Pleasant Publications, 1972.

Lee, James E. "More North of Northampton." *Shoreliner* 21 (no. 1, 1990): 31-33.

Lee, James E. "North of Northampton." *Shoreliner* 20 (no. 2, 1989): 7-19.

Lewis, Edward A. *Vermont's Covered Bridge Road: The Story of the St. Johnsbury & Lamoille County Railroad*. Strasburg, Pa.: Baggage Car, 1974.

Lovett, Robert W. "The Harvard Branch Railroad, 1849-1855." *Railway and Locomotive Historical Society Bulletin* , No. 113 (1965): 43-65.

Massachusetts Executive Office of Transportation and Construction. *Massachusetts State Rail Plan*. Boston: 1976.

McLaughlin, D.W. "Poughkeepsie Gateway." *Railway and Locomotive Historical Society Bulletin* , No. 119 (1968): 6-32.

Mead, Edgar T. *The Up-Country Line: Boston, Concord & Montreal RR to the New Hamshire Lakes and White Mountains*. Brattleboro, Vt.: Stephen Greene Press, 1975.

Mead, Edgar T., Jr. *Through Covered Bridges to Concord: A Recollection of the Concord & Claremont RR (NH)*. Brattleboro, Vt.: Stephen Greene Press, 1970.

Melvin, George. "The Aroostook Valley Railroad." *Railfan & Railroad*, March 1990, 44-50.

Middleton, William. *When the Steam Railroads Electrified*. Milwaukee: Kalmbach Books, 1974.

Moody, Linwood W. *The Maine Two-Footers: The Story of the Two-Foot Gauge Railroads of Maine*. Berkeley, Calif.: Howell-North, 1959.

Nelligan, Tom. "The Rutland Revisited." *Bulletin of the National Railway Historical Society* 34 , no. 3 (1969): 42-43.

Nelligan, Tom. "Whatever Happened to the New Haven?" *Trains*, September 1982, 16-17.

Nevel, Bonnie. *A Guide to America's Rail-Trails*. 5th ed. Washington, D.C.: Rails-to-Trails Conservancy, 1990.

Nevel, Bonnie, and Peter Harnik. *Railroads Recycled: How Local Initiative and Federal Support Launched the Rails-to-Trails Movement 1965-1990*. Washington, D.C.: Rails-to-Trails Conservancy, 1990.

Nielson, Waldo. *Right-of-Way: A Guide to Abandoned Railroads in the United States*. Bend, Ore.: Maverick Publications, 1992.

Northey, Richard P. "A Brief History of the Essex Railroad." *B&M Bulletin* 19, no. 2 (1990): 12-15.

Ozog, Edward J. "Another Way to Boston: The New York & New England in Northern Rhode Island." 3 pts. *Shoreliner* 21 (no. 3, 1990): 28-38; (no. 4, 1990): 6-38; 22 (no. 1, 1991): 23-38.

Pierce, Merle. "The Newport and Wickford Railroad and Steamboat Company." *Shoreliner* 15 (no. 4, 1984): 37-39.

Pinkepank, Jerry A. "Whence the Rutland." *Trains*, May 1964, 39.

Poor, Henry V. *History of the Railroads and Canals of the United States* . . . New York: J.M. Shultz & Co., 1860.

Rhode Island Statewide Planning Program. *Rhode Island State Rail Plan.* Providence: 1977.

Shaughnessy, Jim. *The Rutland Railroad.* Berkeley, Calif.: Howell-North, 1964.

Shaw, Robert B. *A History of Railroad Accidents, Safety Precautions and Operating Practices.* N.p., 1978.

Snow, Glover A. "Meriden, Waterbury & Connecticut River Railroad." *Transportation: Official Publication of the Connecticut Electric Railway Association* 7 (August 1953): 1-37.

Stanford, R. Patrick. *Lines of the New York, New Haven and Hartford Railroad Company.* N.p., 1976.

Stanley, Robert C. *Narrow Gauge: The Story of the Boston, Revere Beach & Lynn Railroad.* BSRA Bulletin 16. Cambridge, Mass.: Boston Street Railroad Association, 1980.

Turner, Gregg M., and Melancthon W. Jacobus, . *Connecticut Railroads: An Illustrated History.* Hartford: Connecticut Historical Society, 1986.

U.S. Department of Transporation. *Final Standards, Classification, and Designation of Lines of Class I Railroads in the U.S.: A Report by the Secretary of Transportation.* 2 vols. Washington, D.C.: Dept. of Transporation, 1977.

U.S. Department of Transportation. *Rail Service in the Midwest and Northeast Region: A Report by the Secretary of Transportation.* 3 vols. Washington, D.C.: Dept. of Transportation, 1974.

U.S. Federal Railroad Administration. *United States Transporation Zone Maps.* 2 vols. Washington, D.C.: Government Printing Office, 1975. Stock no. 050-005-00012-7.

U.S. Interstate Commerce Commission. Rail Services Planning Office. *Evaluation of the U.S. Railway Association's Preliminary System Plan.* Washington, D.C.: Interstate Commerce Commission, 1975.

U.S. Interstate Commerce Commission. Rail Services Planning Office. *The Public Response to the Secretary of Transportation's Rail Service Report: Vol. 1. New England States.* Washington, D.C.: Interstate Commerce Commission, 1974.

U.S. Interstate Commerce Commission. Bureau of Transport Economics and Statistics. *Railroad Abandonments, 1920-1943.* Washington, D.C.: Interstate Commerce Commission, January 1945. Statement no. 453, file no. 136-B-2.

U.S. Railway Association. *Final System Plan for Restructuring Railroads in the Northeast and Midwest Region Pursuant to the Regional Rail Reorganization Act of 1973.* 2 vols.Washington, D.C.: U.S. Railway Association, 1975.

U.S. Railway Association. *Preliminary System Plan for Restructuring Railroads in the Northeast and Midwest Region Pursuant to the Regional Rail Reorganization Act of 1973.* 2 vols. Washington, D.C.: U.S. Railway Association, 1975.

Walker, Harold S. "The Bangor, Oldtown & Milford Railroad, 1836-1869." *Railway and Locomotive Historical Society Bulletin,* No. 106 (1962): 40-48.

Walker, Mike. *Steam Power Video's Comprehensive Railroad Atlas of North America: North East U.S.A.* Kent, England: Steam Powered Publishing, 1993.

Weller, John L. *The New Haven Railroad.* New York: Hastings, 1969.

Withington, Sidney. *The First Twenty Years of Railroading in Connecticut.* New Haven: Yale University Press, 1935. Tercentenary Committee of the State of Connecticut, Publication no. 45.

Wroe, Lewis. "The Hampden Railroad." *Railroad Enthusiast,* November 1959, 2-6.

General Index

abandoned railroads
  conversion to recreational trails, 66
  ownership, 66-67
Agawam Junction, MA, 48
Air Line Limited, 44
Air-Line Railroad
  See Boston & New York Air-Line Railroad
Albion, ME, 62
Alder Stream, ME , 61
Allerton Farms, CT, 45
Amtrak, 38
Atwood, Ellis D., 63
automobiles, effect on railroads, 36
Ayer, MA, 50, 52-53

Bangor & Aroostook Railroad, 35-36, 63
Bangor & Piscataquis Railroad, 63
Beacon, NY, 46
Bedford. MA, 60
Bellows Falls, VT, 57-58
Bennington & Rutland Railroad, 57-58
Bennington, VT, 58
Berlin, MA, 55-56
Bigelow, ME, 61
Billerica & Bedford Railroad, 59-60
Billerica, MA, 59
Blackstone Canal, 49
Blackstone, MA, 42, 45

Boston & Albany Railroad, 35-38, 46, 48, 53-54
  Winchendon Branch, 55
Boston & Lowell Railroad, 34-35, 54, 60
Boston & Maine Railroad, 34-35, 37-38, 47-48, 51-55, 58, 60, 70
  Worcester, Nashua & Portland division, 51, 53, 55
Boston & New York Air-Line Railroad, 43-45
Boston & New York Central Railroad, 34, 42, 44-45
Boston & Providence Railroad, 34-35
Boston & Worcester Railroad, 34, 49
Boston, Concord & Montreal Railroad, 35
Boston, Hartford & Erie Railroad, 42-43
Boston, MA, 33-34, 42, 45, 54-55, 58
Brewster, NY, 43
Bridgeport, CT, 44
Bridgton & Harrison Railroad, 62-63
Bridgton & Saco River Railroad, 61-62
Bridgton, ME, 62
Bristol, CT, 42
Brookline, MA, 43
Bunker Hill Monument, 33

Burlington, VT, 56-58
Burnham, ME, 62

Canaan, CT, 46, 49
Carrabasset, ME, 61
Central Massachusetts Railroad, 35, 54-56
Central New England & Western Railroad, 46
Central New England Railway, 47-49
Central Vermont Railroad, 57-58
Central Vermont Railway, 36, 55
Champlain & Connecticut River Railroad, 56-57
Charles River Railroad, 43
Charlestown, MA, 33
Chester, VT, 57
Clematis Brook, MA, 56
Clinton, MA, 55
cog railways, 70
Columbia, CT, 46
Connecticut Western Railroad, 46, 54
Conrail, 38-39, 46, 49, 70
Coventry, RI, 45

Danbury, CT, 43
Dedham, MA, 42
Delaware & Hudson Railroad, 38
Dorchester, MA, 42
Dutchess & Columbia Railroad, 46

Eastern Railroad, 34, 51
Edaville Railroad, 59, 63
electric railroads, 69
Epping, NH, 52-53
Essex County, MA, 34

Federal (train), 47
Feeding Hills, MA, 48
Fitchburg & Worcester Railroad , 50
Fitchburg Railroad, 35, 46, 50, 53-54, 58
Franklin & Megantic Railroad, 60-61
Franklin County, ME, 60
Franklin, MA, 45
Fremont, NH, 52-53

Gardiner, ME, 62
Ghost Train, 44
Gonic, NH, 52
Granite Railway, 33

Green Mountain Flyer, 58
Green Mountain Railroad, 58
Griffins, CT, 49
Groton Junction, MA, 50
Groton, MA, 67
Guilford Transportation Industries, 38-39, 46

Harrisburg Day Express, 47
Harrisburg, PA, 54
Harrison, ME, 62
Hartford & Connecticut Western Railroad, 46
Hartford, CT, 35, 41-42, 45-46, 49
Hartford, Providence & Fishkill Railroad, 41-46
Hawleyville, CT, 45
Hazelhurst, MA, 59
Hollis, NH, 52-53, 67
Hudson, MA, 55
Hudson, NH, 52
Hurricane of 1938, 55

inclines, 70
industrial railroads, 70
industrial spurs, 70
Interstate Commerce Commission (I.C.C.), 36, 52, 58

Jeffersons, MA, 54

Kennebec & Wiscasset Railroad, 62
Kennebec Central, ME, 62-63
Kingfield & Dead River Railroad, 61
Kingfield, ME, 61

Lakeville, CT, 49
Langtown, ME, 61
Lawrence, MA, 35, 50
logging railroads, 70
Lowell, MA, 35, 50

Madrid, ME, 60
Maine Central Railroad, 35-36, 38, 60-62
Maine Narrow Gauge Railroad & Museum, 63
Manchester, CT, 46
Mansfield, George E., 59-60
maps, 65
Marbles, ME, 61

Massachusetts Bay Transportation Authority (MBTA), 55, 70
Massachusetts Central Railroad, 54
McLeod. A. A., 47, 54
Mellon, Timothy, 38
Metro North Commuter Railroad, 38
Middletown, CT, 43-45
Midland Railroad , 42
Millerton, NY, 46
Monson Junction, ME, 63
Monson Railroad, 63
Monson Slate Company, 63
Monson, ME, 63
Montpelier, VT, 57
Morgan, J. P., 47
Mount Royal (train), 58
Mt. Abram, ME, 61

Nashua & Lowell Railroad, 50
Nashua & Rochester Railroad, 50, 52-53
Nashua, NH, 50-53
New Barre Plains, MA, 55
New England Limited , 44
New Haven Railroad
   See New York, New Haven & Hartford Railroad
New Haven, CT, 43-44, 46
New Haven, Middletown & Willimantic Railroad , 43
New York & New England Railroad, 35, 41, 43-45, 47
New York & New Haven Railroad, 34
New York Central Railroad, 37, 58
New York, New Haven & Hartford Railroad, 35, 37-38, 43-45, 47-48, 54
New York, NY, 58
Newton, MA, 34
Norfolk County Railroad, 42
North Billerica, MA, 60
North Windham, CT, 45
Northampton, MA, 54-56
Northern Railroad, 35
Norwich & Worcester Railroad, 49

Oakdale, MA, 55
Old Colony Railroad, 35

Penn Central Railroad, 37, 45, 49, 70
Pepperell, MA, 52, 67

Philadelphia & Reading Railroad, 47
Philadelphia, Reading & New England Railroad, 47
Phillips & Rangley Railroad, 61
Phillips, ME, 60-61
Pinsly, Samuel M., 52
Plainfield, CT, 42, 45
Pomfret, CT, 45
Portland & Rochester Railroad, 50-53
Portland, CT, 45
Portland, ME, 34, 50-53, 63
Poughkeepsie, NY, 46-48, 54
Providence & Plainfield Railroad, 41
Providence & Worcester Railroad, 49
Providence, RI, 41-42, 45
Putnam, CT, 43, 45

Quincy, MA, 33

Randolph, ME, 62
Rangley, ME, 60-61
Readville, MA, 42
Rhinecliff, NY, 46
Rochester, NH, 50-52
Rouses Point, NY, 57
Rutland & Burlington Railroad, 57
Rutland Railroad, 35-37, 56-59, 70
Rutland, MA, 55
Rutland, VT, 58

Salem, MA, 34-35
Sandy River & Rangley Lake Railroad, 61, 63
Sandy River Railroad, 60-61
Sanford & Eastern Railroad, 52
Shirley, MA, 67
Simsbury, CT, 49
South Berwick, ME, 50
South Carver, MA, 59, 63
South Sudbury, MA, 55
Southbridge & Blackstone Railroad, 42
Southbury, CT, 45
Sprague, Phineas, Jr., 63
Springfield, MA, 35, 46, 48-49
Steamtown USA , 58
Sterling Junction, MA, 50
Strong, ME, 60
Sudbury, MA, 53

Tarrifville, CT, 46, 48
Togus, ME, 62
tram lines, 69
Troy, NY, 58

United States Geological Survey, 65

Vermont Central Railroad, 57
Vermont Central Railway, 35
Vermont Railway, 58

Wachusett Reservoir, 55
Walpole Railroad, 42
Walpole, MA, 42
Waltham North, MA , 56
Washington, DC, 54
Waterbury, CT, 41-43, 45
Waterville, ME, 62
Wayland & Sudbury Branch Railroad, 53-54
Wayland, MA, 53
West Berlin, MA, 55
Westbrook, ME, 52

Western Railroad , 49
Western Vermont Railroad, 57
Weston, MA, 53-54
Wheelwright, MA, 55-56
White River Junction, VT, 57
White Train, 44
Willimantic, CT, 42-46
Winslow, ME, 62
Winsted, CT, 46
Wiscasset & Quebec Railroad, 62
Wiscasset, ME, 62
Wiscasset, Waterville & Farmington Railroad, 62
Woonsocket, RI, 43
Worcester & Nashua Railroad, 49-51, 53
Worcester, MA, 49, 51-53
Worcester, Nashua & Rochester Railroad, 50-53

York & Cumberland Railroad, 50

About the Author

RONALD DALE KARR, a reference librarian at the University of Massachusetts Lowell, holds a Ph.D. in History from Boston University. He is a graduate of Bucknell University and also holds an M.S. in Library Science from Simmons College. A longtime railfan himself, he previously worked at the U.S. Department of Transportation in Cambridge, Mass., and at the Northwestern University Transportation Library in Evanston, Ill. He has authored numerous historical articles, as well as another Rail Heritage book, *The Rail Lines of Southern New England* (1995), also published by Branch Line Press.

Also by Ronald Dale Karr

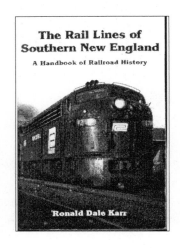

The Rail Lines of Southern New England

A Handbook of Railroad History

Ronald Dale Karr

"Provides brief yet thorough summaries on the predecessor rail lines of the region and tells what remains of them today."
—*Railfan & Railroad*

"This is a wonderful compilation of information on the rail lines of southern New England. . . . Anyone with an interest in the history of any railroad line in the region should consult this important and valuable book."
—*Historical Journal of Massachusetts*

"Anyone interested in New England railroads should have this book."
—*Trains Magazine*

384 pages ❖ nearly 90 illustrations ❖ maps ❖ 6" × 9" ❖ $22.95

Available from your local bookstore or hobby shop, or order direct from

Branch Line Press
13 Cross St.
Pepperell, MA 01463
(508) 433-2236

All orders must be prepaid by check or money order.
Please include $3.00 shipping & handling for first copy; $1.50 for each additional copy. MA residents: please add $1.15 sales tax per copy.